THE LOST AIRFIELDS OF ANGUS

Jean,
Best Wishes'.

Margaret G. Bowman

Margaret G. Bowman

Bruce Clark Printers, Dundee

ISBN – 978-1-7398200-0-8

British Library Cataloguing-in-Publication Data. A catalogue record of this book is available on request from the British Library.

First published in Great Britain 2021

Bruce Clark Printers

Caldron Works

St Salvador Street

Dundee

DD3 7EU

www.info@bruceclark.co.uk

Book Set Design – blacklinestudios.co.uk

Book Cover Design – Rikki Craig

Photograph - Wikimedia Commons/Public Domain

This book is dedicated to the memory of those who risked their lives to preserve the freedom of this nation in World Wars I and II.

MG Bowman - 2021

CONTENTS

THE LOST AIRFIELDS OF ANGUS

INTRODUCTION

'Our task is not to win the battle - but to win the war'

- Prime Minister Winston Chruchill in his broadcast 19th May 1942

Why Angus? ....I have lived in the county for the greater part of my life, my own family were raised here and it is where I call 'home'. I am now a writer, primarily of feature articles, published in many of the history and nostalgic genre magazines that grace the shelves of newsstands.

It was one bleak winters morning whilst driving along a narrow country road that skirts the old local airfield, an old Nissen hut attracted my attention. It lies adjacent to an equally old, corrugated iron hangar, now used as a storage area for farm machinery. I felt myself drawn to their neglected, haunting derelict state and reflected on their purpose during wartime hostilities. This area would have been exceptionally busy, and these, now derelict, buildings would have played a vital role in the defence of our nation. The triumphs and tragedies of the mostly young men and women, courageously rebelling against aggressive enemy forces stirred my passion for knowledge and here my quest started.

Uncovering vast amounts of research material, I knew from an early stage this would be a much greater task than at first anticipated. As my research progressed, the journey took me on a far wider course than I intended to cover.

Local aviation and technology leaders featured as part of my research, with Angus having its own revolutionary innovators, some whom are now largely forgotten and relatively unknown, even to residents of the region.

Close to the county lies the city of Dundee which is situated on the River Tay estuary, best known for its 'Jam; Jute and Journalism'. Due to its proximity to the Angus County boundary, this locale played a substantial wartime role being a site of shipbuilding and docks. Dundee and the county of Angus, like the most of the United Kingdom, were no strangers to having individuals who were willing to commit espionage, providing the enemy with information for their advantage. Whilst searching through archived material, two significant traitors emerged who shocked local residents. I could not resist adding their narratives in a later chapter. There may have been others, but none quite as remarkable as their high-profile accounts.

The arrival of a prominent Russian Diplomat at the small air station of RAF Tealing, would give today's 'fake news' a completely new meaning. The variety of information in reports, many being personal narratives, was indeed substantial and it was not until military accounts were released recently, that the 'true' details of the visit came to light. The county of Angus played a foremost position in Churchill's deception planning, also in having RAF Fordoun air station based just out with the county boundary holding a fleet of 'dummy aircraft' giving the enemy an impression of the country's preparation for an invasion assignment.

The threat from enemy attack over Angus was substantial and many of our coastal areas suffered structural damage with loss of life, but without the magnificent effects of our defences and the courage and skill of our airmen, the outcome of WWI and WWII could have been very different. The sacrifices they made were not in vain.

CHAPTER 1
EARLY SCOTTISH AVIATORS

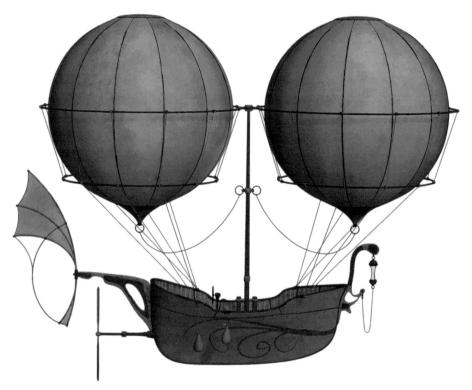

Photograph - Pixabay Images

CHAPTER 1
EARLY SCOTTISH AVIATORS

'I have not the smallest molecule of faith in aerial navigation,
other than ballooning' - Lord Kelvin

The desire for flight has been an all-consuming quest for man.   The freedom and opportunity to view the land from a different dimension and travel distances, developed a culture of innovation over centuries. This led to a frenzy of inventors, all with one vision and ultimate common goal –the achievement of flight.

It was an Angus man, James Tytler who is recognised as the first British person to fly in a hot air balloon of his own design – *'The Edinburgh Fire Balloon,'* in 1784. Tytler was born in the old Manse at Fern, near Brechin in 1745 and was educated at the University of Edinburgh where he studied medicine and held various positions, in which he was less than successful.

Financial issues left him with mounting debts and he attempted several times to take refuge over the border. One of his more successful ventures which eliminated his debt problems, was to write and have published, a book detailing the expertise of Edinburgh's 'ladies of the night' which not surprisingly became a bestseller. However, rising debts, compounded by possessing a colourful lifestyle, necessitated he took work as a pharmacist, preacher and artist while he continued his writing, which included editorial work with The Encyclopaedia Britannica. This was where his interest in flight was stimulated. He read about the achievements of the Montgolfier brothers and set upon creating his own air-borne mission.

James Tytler – Unknown Artist at Wikimedia Commons/Public Domain

He designed and built his balloon, which was structured like a wine cask and was charcoal fired. Its maiden flight was scheduled for the 25th August 1784. Unfortunately, on that attempt it flew only a few feet off the ground, however, two days later he achieved success. He set off his balloon again from Comely Gardens in Edinburgh, reaching a height of approximately 350ft and it travelled at least, half of a mile. Cheered on as a hero by watching crowds who gathered to witness the event, but unfortunately this was short lived. Subsequent attempts were dismally unsuccessful and Tytler went on to other ventures, eventually finding his way to the United States where he ended his days miserably, subsequent to alcohol abuse.

His memorable Edinburgh flight accomplishment however, successfully made entry to the history annals where he has been credited as the first Briton to fly in a hot air balloon in 1784. This was commemorated on his

3

bicentenary year in 1984, with Post Office first day covers. A replica of his extraordinary balloon and flying events, was also held in the gardens of Holyrood in the Scottish capital recognising Tytler as a national hero rather than a rogue and a rascal, as his background would suggest.

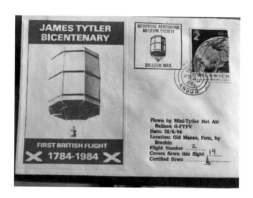

First Day Cover - James Tytler's Balloon Flight – Writers Own Material

The race for flight was now on but a century at least would pass before manned, sustained flight which could be controlled, would be achieved.

Closer to home, Scotland had a less well-known aviation pioneer, Preston Watson, son of a prominent Dundee businessman. He started his career by joining his father who was a partner in the prestigious firm of Watson and Philip Wholesalers, but acquired a keen interest in the progression of mechanical activities, specifically with manned flight. His formative education was at Dundee High School, thereafter at University College Dundee where he studied engineering. He swiftly realised that if aviation was to be his chosen career pathway, he would have to create his own research, as little was published on aerodynamics for him to learn from.   Recognised for being the designer of a '*motorised heavier-than-air flying machine*' in 1903, his first flight was taken at Errol Airfield, near to Dundee. Unfortunately, little factual evidence was documented in relation to the exact date and technical aspects of the episode, except eye-witness accounts which cannot be used solely to substantiate the event. There are also claims that indicate the aircraft used was more in terms of a 'glider' format. Watson did however, go on to build a further two flying machines and also invented a '*rocking ring system for control*'

4

which he successfully patented in 1909. His No2 aircraft successfully achieved powered flight in 1910, using a Humber engine, which validated his aeronautical theories.

Watson had innovative plans for his No3 aircraft, but on the outbreak of WWI, put these on hold when he applied for a commission with the Royal Naval Air Service (RNAS). Following formal flying instruction, he was awarded the Royal Aero Club Certificate on the 16th March 1915 - his licence to fly.

On the 30th June, Flight Sub-Lieutenant Preston Watson of the RNAS, was on a routine flight between Eastchurch in Kent to Eastbourne in East Sussex His aircraft abruptly lost control mid-flight and crashed, killing him on impact. He is buried in the Western Cemetery in Dundee – only 34 years old.

Replica of Preston Watsons Flying Machine in Dundee Museum of Transport 2019 – Writers Own Photograph

His younger brother James, some fifty years later, pursued the claim that Preston had taken the *'first powered, controlled, sustainable, heavier-than-air flight'* prior to the Wright brothers, but with a lack of documentary and photographic evidence, the case was dismissed. The name of Preston Watson, however, continues to live on. A street is named after him in Errol Village, in memory of his achievements and a replica of his early aircraft has been meticulously constructed by members of Dundee's Model Aircraft Club which now *'flies'* in the Dundee Museum of Transport. Preston never lived to tell his story or lay claim to making the first powered flight but he certainly holds the title of being one of the first *'Flying Scotsmen'*.

There were many European inventors of an early form of aircraft as we would recognise today, but it was another pair of siblings, this time across the Atlantic who were to be credited with the first controlled aircraft flight. The Wright brothers, Wilbur and Orville, were the two American aviation pioneers who were recognised as inventing, building and flying the first controlled, powered, sustained, manned flight with their *'Wright Flyer'* on 17th December 1903 in North Carolina.

Britain's first military pilot was Scots born, Bertram Dickson. He holds the distinction of being the first British serviceman to qualify as a pilot in April, 1910. Dickson lobbied the War Office to let him demonstrate the advantages of using aircraft for effective ground observation. His life came to an unfortunate end in 1913 following injuries which were sustained previously in an aircraft accident.

It was another Scotsman who was influential with the development of the formation of an Air Force. David Henderson, who attended Glasgow University at the age of 15 to study engineering then trained at Sandhurst, was commissioned then joined the Argyll and Sutherland Highlanders. By the age of 49, he learned to fly. In 1912, he was the adviser to the Air Committee, which established the Royal Flying Corps by April of that year, initially as a part of the British Army, whose purpose was to investigate the military potential of this new phenomenon of manned flight.

Post WWI saw a surge in British Aviation endeavours with the advancement of engineering technology allowing longer distance flying. On the 13th December 1918, Sergeant Thomas Brown from Penicuik, south of Edinburgh, participated as one of the flight crew on such a flight to India, along with a dog called Tiny. Brown was a carpenter then a draughtsman, prior to serving in the RFC from 1915, thereafter, the RAF. Setting off from Britain, in a Handley Page V/1500 Bi-plane called *'Old Carthusian,'* passing through the Mediterranean to North Africa then onto the Middle East, their goal was finally achieved landing at Karachi.

The journey took a month and was not without some considerable challenges, but the six-man crew, four of whom were from Scotland, certainly achieved their long-haul pioneering mission.

The competition then was fierce with young aviation pioneers attempting to fly further, higher and faster than previously.

CHAPTER 2
THE ANGUS AIRFIELDS

'Never in the field of human conflict was so much owed by so many to so few' - **Winston Churchill, 20th August 1940 House of Commons**

Aircraft commercial potential was starting to be recognised, but in the early 20th century the potential for military use was being explored. In November 1911, Lord Haldane the then Secretary for State for War, proposed creating a British Aeronautical Service with a Naval Wing, Military Wing and a Central Flying School Created from this proposal, the Royal Flying Corps, (RFC) was established in April 1912, commencing with five squadrons and by the end of 1913, Winston Churchill, the First Lord of the Admiralty, announced the independent status of the Naval Wing, then classified as the Royal Naval Air Service – RNAS.

There was initial confusion relating to the responsibility of each service. Following opportunistic Zeppelin raids from Germany plus the sinking of the passenger liner, Lusitania off the coast of Ireland by German submarines, it became clear that operational patrols, reconnaissance and defence was now the priority.

In 1916, the War Office formed a Home Defence Scheme which recognised that searchlights, anti-aircraft guns and fighter aircraft were now required to protect our island nation from marauding German attacks. WWI was not only a war of attrition in the trenches fought in Europe, the danger was now crossing the North Sea, bringing the war to Britain. The RFC then took over the responsibility for the air defence role – and so it began.

Why select the county of Angus as a suitable military airfield zone? In many ways, Angus is perfectly situated being on the east coast of Scotland, mainly agricultural with its largest populated areas hugging the coastline. Angus is an area which would not raise the interest of enemy forces, as there are few heavy industrial sites to be seen as a danger and therefore be eliminated,

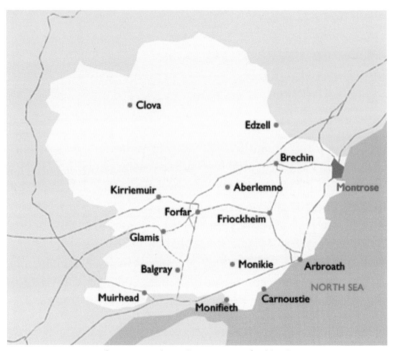

Map of Angus - Wikimedia Commons/public domain

It is a county which is situated closer to Norway than to the Home Counties in England and ideally placed for defence of the Orkney and Shetland Isles. It sounds like a pretty *'safe'* and quiet area but like all equations, there is a negative side. On the east-side of the county, there is the North Sea and to the west-northwest, the Grampian mountains.

Many of the airfields, in particular by the time of WWII, were located in the narrow geographical band of land in-between. Ideal for the training of novice pilots providing significant landing challenges, especially at night, but also secure enough for maintenance, essential repair and rebuilding of aircraft.

The coastal airfields were ideally placed to be deck-landing practice areas and also act as satellite bases for the major military and air service sites at Dundee and Montrose.

Coastal Command units were in action from Scotland from the first days of war until the last, with Angus airfields playing a major role in both world wars in defence. The sites were operating as pilot training bases, predominately in 1914-18, with vital maritime roles during WWII. Training for novice pilots was a necessary function as the regions' airfields were reasonably safe from air attack, unlike the south of England where defence against enemy bombing raids took priority.

WORLD WAR I SITES

RFC/RAF Montrose – Scotland's first military airfield from 1913

RFC/RAF Auldbar - Airship Mooring site – satellite landing area for RAF Longside,   Peterhead - 1918- 1919

RNAS Dundee –   Stannergate – from 1914 – 1919 - Seaplane Base

British Army/RNAS Barry Buddon – training infantry during Boer War years- Trench training WWI also the satellite site for Stannergate Dundee from 1915 - 1919

RAF Edzell –   Satellite site for Montrose from 1918 -1919

WORLD WAR II SITES

RAF Montrose – 1936 – 1952 -Currently Montrose Air Station Heritage Centre

RNAS Arbroath – 1939 – As HMS Condor - currently RM Condor Base

RNAS Easthaven – As HMS Peewit from 1943 – 1946

RAF Edzell - 1930's operated as a civilian airfield then military 1940 -1950 thereafter used as a motor racing circuit until 1960, used then by USN as part of High Frequency Direction Finding network (HFDF) until eventual closure in 1997.

RAF Kinnell - 1942- 1945

RAF Stracathro – 1941 – Taken over by Edzell in 1945

RAF Tealing –1942 – 1948

Barry Buddon – Satellite for Dundee and currently Barry Buddon Army Training Centre

HMS Ambrose Royal Naval Submarine Base Dundee – 1940 – 1946

RNAS Seaplane Base as HMS Condor II at Dundee Stannergate 1940 - 1944

RAF Woodhaven – Fife – Seaplane base on River Tay

CHAPTER 3
AIR STATIONS AND AIR FORCE EVOLUTION

*'....the battle of France is over. I expect that the Battle of
Britain is to begin...'* - **Winston Churchill 18th June 1940
House of Commons**

1911 – 1918 WORLD WAR I YEARS

The selection of a suitable site for use as an RFC airfield, was made by
the Officers who would be the users. The military authorities designated
an area, roughly where they would want it to be located but it was their
mission to find the best situation.

The buildings required varied vastly depending on the size and locality
but they were generally designed to house four main groups: ***Officers Mess
and Quarters***; A ***Regimental*** building which included accommodation
for administration. ***Technical buildings*** – hangars; stores; maintenance
etc and also a ***Women's hostel*** – for the female staff working on-site.

The number of aeroplane sheds and hangars depended largely on when
the station was built, the number of flights and the number of squadrons
based on the site. Hangars were originally called '*sheds*' except in the
case when tents were used as hangars e.g., the *Bessoneau hangar.* This
was the first standard transportable hangar of the time and remains of
the mooring posts can still be found. The introduction of the Anderson

Belfast trusses for use on more substantial end-opening aircraft sheds, made it possible for them to be linked together allowing multiple spans as can be seen at Montrose whose 'sheds' date from 1913.

In 1918, the War Committee was established to 'firm up' Home Defence, and it was recommended that the RFC and the RNAS become amalgamated. It was on the 1st April 1918 that the Royal Air Force was created.

THE IN-BETWEEN WAR YEARS - 'THE EXPANSION PERIOD'

This period of time was also known for its greatest turmoil and was fraught with difficulties in socio-economical terms until the latter end of the 1930's, when the drive for change was forced once again on this country.

In terms of aviation, the period following the Great War was transformational. The aeroplane was now far better designed and its manufacture had become industrialised. Commercial air services became the new and exciting form of transport with new routes open for exploration. Flying was a seen as a romantic, glamorous and dangerous means of transportation and airships were still seen as a safe and pleasant passenger conveyance, until the Hindenburg airship disaster in 1937.

In the following years, Hitler advanced his plans utilising his state finances to rearm his fighting strength, building warships, forming an air supremacy by manufacturing aircraft on a massive scale, weaponry with tanks, bombs, all solving the unemployment situation, yet building up the Germanic empire.

During this time, Britain and France were taking a much slower pace to recovery. The politicians were aware of Hitler's motives but neither country had any appetite to intervene at this time. Memories of the previous conflict were still too painful and further discord would not be welcomed.

Throughout these dramatic years, the RAF started to expand its air stations in response and by 1935 had four specialised commands: Bomber; Fighter; Coastal and Training. Due to the complex administration of such

13

a structure, the RAF passed over command and control of the Fleet Air Arm to the Royal Navy and plans to secure defence of the nation were once again put into action.

This time, the planning of additional airfield sites in the best practical locations and with the best organisation of runways, storage, necessary buildings, access and all necessary logistics were identified at Command level. This was a far more structured approach to every detail. It specified that, 'runways should provide full length runs from every direction. Design should be either rectangular or square' to enable pilots' to perform premium, swift, take-off and landings.'

Since WWI, the design of aircraft had changed dramatically and the grass landing sites previously used were of no longer use. The aircraft undercarriage retracting gear of WWII aircraft would be clogged up with mud, building up on the mechanical parts, plus stones being thrown up damaging the propellers. Metal tracking; Army and Somerfield track; Square Mesh and Pierced Steel Plank (an American Track) were used as well as concrete/ tarmac runways and perimeter tracks for taxi-ing aircraft.

Hangars for aircraft storage and maintenance were now being developed rapidly and many types were being created to suited the purpose of the air stations. As seen from their use in WWI, transportable hangars were invaluable therefore, the Air Ministry in 1936, indicated a standard easy to erect, end-opening with doors at either end, with minimal permanent foundations for use in war, be manufactured. The Bellman hangar was mass produced as well as the Callendar-Hamilton type, a similar design being manufactured for the RNAS.

Many of the buildings were of concrete construction, primarily due to the shortage of bricklayers, but also to accommodate the protection necessary against bomb blast. The design of the airfield now included far more technical buildings, with hangars; fuel stores; heating and electricity supplies, workshops, married quarters; guardroom and watch tower, (later to be known as Watch Office) Special arrangements to house the bomb store and armoury were made on each site, obviously at a distance from the main base.

14

1939 – 1945 WORLD WAR II

At 11am on Sunday 3rd September 1939, Neville Chamberlain informed the citizens of Britain on his radio broadcast, that following the invasion of Poland, Britain and France had declared war on Nazi Germany. WWII had begun.

Concentrated bombing was expected, as Britain was now an easy target to reach by German aircraft, unlike the previous war. Designated planes were equipped to cause maximum damage and airfields took the precaution of having a more dispersed layout for new air stations with the technical buildings set mostly apart from the rest. The permanent buildings of the expansion period were not economical in terms of cost or construction time, therefore *'temporary'* buildings were manufactured and assembled as the likelihood of war was anticipated and rapid erection of vital structures on military sites was now a priority.

Standard building designs took shape taking cognisance of the rapidly changing development of aircraft designs, their equipment and weaponry. More workshop and maintenance areas were necessary with additional space also designated for communications with aircrew relating to missions.

Parachutes had been part of the aircrew's standard equipment since 1927 and each member had to be measured for and issued with, his own parachute which had to be inspected on a monthly basis. Condensation was a major problem, and to prevent them shrinking, they had to be dried in a specifically designed building which met the requirements of drying; inspection; packing and storage, which must be dust free and temperature controlled. These buildings usually had a lobby with an inner and outer door to prevent loss of heat, control of dust and be of sufficient height to accommodate the parachute being hung from the top with the rigging laid out on long tables before packing.

By the time WWII commenced, there was a new generation of fighter pilots, no stranger to the horrors of war. They grew up in the shadow of it and under several years of the mounting prospect of yet another conflict, there were no shortage of aircrew volunteers.

The bi-planes of the previous war period were now replaced with new monoplanes, notably the Hawker Hurricane and Supermarine Spitfire which were to become the 'heroes' of WWII. It is acknowledged in Dilip Sarkar's '*Spitfire Voices*' that '*to become a fighter pilot was the ambition of most volunteers but to be a Spitfire pilot was their ultimate aim.*'

Hurricane and Spitfires - R Macdonald Chelmsford - Wikimedia Commons/Public Domain

Hangars and aircraft sheds were required now in vast numbers and a variety were produced to meet the demands. As the early war years started to bite, the need for temporary hangars became crucial and requirement for a high-water tower to be sited alongside was essential in the case of fire. Often in the more rural airfield sites, blister type hangar (a form of open ended temporary covered shed) was enough to protect visibility from reconnaissance.

Bomb stores with blast walls were rapidly erected and situated at a distance for obvious reasons. Station armoury buildings also held accommodation for lecture rooms, photographic laboratories, classrooms for practical instruction, among others for teaching and training.

Aircrew training was more advanced than in the WWI years, with training for fighter pilots taking a new format established in 1939, now in four stages. **Initial Training Wing** – theory of flight and basic training:

Elementary Flying School – advanced theory and flying on training aircraft: **Service Flying Training** – advanced aircraft training – this is where the pilot got their *Wings*: finally, the **Operational Training Unit** – this was where pilots met up with navigators, Observers, Gunners and Wireless Operators. Training units also had synthetic training via a **Link Trainer** often known as *the blue box,* which was an early form of flight simulation invented by pioneer aviator, Edwin Link in 1929.

Military Personnel using Link Trainer - R Y Richie Flickr - Wikimedia Commons/Public Domain

The synthetic navigational classroom was housed in brick buildings specifically for training all aspects of navigation. There were many airfields with particular training requirements - bombing, torpedo sighting, night flying etc. Use of temporary buildings for a camera obscura; anti-aircraft dome trainers; ambulance and many more were rapidly erected to ensure the young trainees were as prepared and best equipped as possible.

More permanent buildings were generally required for use as barracks but not always depending on the sites use each being unique in design yet with a standard of requirement. Buildings consisted of Officers' Mess and Quarters; Sergeants' Mess and Quarters, WAAFs' Quarters and communal site and included NAAFI; ration stores etc.

Each airfield however, did have a Gas Decontamination building. Despite the declaration that the use of gas in war was prohibited in the Geneva Gas Protocol of 1925, its production and further development was not, therefore in the event of an attack, personnel affected could receive decontamination and early first aid treatment. This building was designed to deal with the forms of gas agents used in WWI, such as lachrymatory, respiratory and blister agents. Gasmasks carried by all civilian and military personnel were an immediate response action, should the occasion arise.

During the late years of the expansion period, speed of production and economy of resources necessitated the use of temporary equivalents to brick and concrete for essential building requirements. By 1940, the Nissen hut system of construction proved to be the most economical and easily transportable. With half-brick walls and spans of 16-28 feet its pre-fabricated half cylindrical corrugated steel shell could be swiftly erected. Designed during WWI by engineer, Major Peter Nissen from a building in Ontario, Canada, they were used extensively in WWII.

Nissen Hut at Arbroath – photograper's own – 2019 (demolished in 2021)

Precast concrete huts also became available between 1941-1944 for specialised uses and camouflage was applied to huts on airfields liable to be attacked with incendiary protection were necessary.

Military airfields had their own shelters mostly constructed of brick or concrete covered with soil and turf as be 'invisible' from the air. Many remain in situ and there are several very good examples still standing. In airfields where the officers mess and quarters were situated in established country houses requisitioned for the purpose, brick shelters above ground or long concrete **'Stanton'** shelters with ventilation ports, escape hatches and blast walls were situated in the grounds, surrounded by trees and shrubs. Manufactured by the Stanton Ironworks Company Nottingham, these shelters could accommodate fifty people.

RAF Edzell Stanton Air Raid Shelter with Blast Wall - photograph courtesy of M Craib

Fighter Command and Bomber Command each had their own requirements for the base allocated, as did Training and Coastal Command.

Watch Offices were of different styles and RNAS had control Towers, the majority of which were built by RM Engineers to a standard design with an integrated crash tender garage. These towers were usually four storeys with office accommodation and meteorology room. Examples of existing structures are included in later chapters.

From the early days of radar at the end of the 1930's, the Radar Reporting System provided early warning of incoming enemy aircraft, through the advantage of Chain Home and Chain Home Low stations. These Radar stations had receiving and directional masts capable of detecting and tracking enemy forces. Air stations had their own radar workshop included in their technical building structure.

Chain Home Radar Control Bunker St Cyrus - photograph courtesy of M Craib

Defence of the airfields against marauders was essential and each airfield had its own underground Battle Headquarters. Pillboxes and Turrets were usually situated on the airfield boundary and provided the fire power when under attack. The retractable pillbox was given the priority for defence such as the Pickett-Hamilton Fort as was the Allan Williams steel turret which was mounted on a curved rail which allowed 360° movement and line of fire. A Tett turret was of similar design with the dome being made of reinforced concrete.

RAF Fighter Command Pickett-Hamilton Retractable Fort – G Woodbine RAF Photographer –

CH17890 IWM - Wikimedia Commons/Public Domain

Although resources were stretched and the preparation time limited, Britain's military and civilian forces were primed and equipped for the grim task ahead of them. Some innovative, astute thinking, as well as courage and gritty spirit of the nation's citizens meant this war would be very different from the last. This small rural part of Scotland, situated hundreds of miles away from the most vulnerable and exposed major cities, towns and villages that line the south coast of Britain in the 'firing line' of enemy attacks, played a vital role in both World Wars.

The geographical location of Angus was ideally placed for the preparation and training of pilots and aircrew, reconnaissance missions, maintenance and rebuilding of damaged aircraft, observation and intelligence communications, surveillance and most importantly. Air and sea defence of our country at war.

Major Burke - Taken in 1913 - Photo courtesy of Alan Doe

21

CHAPTER 4

MONTROSE - SCOTLAND'S FIRST AIR STATION

'Flying Training Command – Flying Instructors School'

56°43'48° N 2°27'05°W

'Red Lichtie' Spitfire outside RAF Montrose Headquarters - Photograph Writers own - 2019

With tensions growing in Europe during the first decade of the new century, First Lord of the Admiralty, Winston Churchill envisaged unimaginable difficulties ahead. He predicted Germany would pose a military threat to the North Sea and claimed that the British Fleet, based at the natural deep-water port at Scapa Flow and the naval bases at Rosyth and Cromarty, required additional protection against enemy attack.

Montrose was ideally placed being located between the naval bases and sitting at the edge of the north-east coastline of Scotland. Montrose became the first operational military airfield in Scotland, also the first in Britain from 1912. Its task was to protect the seaboard from enemy advances and perform reconnaissance missions. At this time; aircraft were still a relatively new concept for military use and their capabilities were still to be fully explored. The threat of airships remained a dangerous force, despite their slow movement and ability to manoeuvre in poor weather conditions. They could sustain longer-distance sorties and remain a continued threat. An appropriate location was sought as a matter of urgency for these new bi-planes to land and take-off safely.

The original airfield was situated at Upper Dysart Farm, south of Montrose, close to Lunan Bay. This became the base for the RFC No 2 Squadron in February 1913 under the command of Major C.J. Burke, who was a creative thinker in terms of the military's use of aircraft. Given it was only a handful of years since the Wright brothers first flight, aeronautical attack and defence was still very much in its infancy. Burke, however could see the immense potential where others could not. He realised the importance aircraft were destined to play in the future of air attack and defence. He was not the best pilot around, being almost as famous for his impressive crashes. He was considered to be *'single minded, yet utterly courageous, determined and held a formidable* sense *of character'*. Major Burke trained his squadron in aerial reconnaissance and also ensured the aircraft were upgraded to carry munitions, in preparation for future combat.

Upper Dysart circa 1913 - Wikimedia Commons/Public Domain

The air station was an elementary set up, with grass landing and the use of tents for accommodation and maintenance. The site, although widespread and open, had a slope which was not the best surface for take-offs and landings of these delicate looking, yet surprisingly robust, flying machines.

Training for pilots was a major function for the air station, as was the varying types of patrols and reconnaissance missions. No 2 Squadron continued to pioneer longer distance flights which was noted as being quite remarkable for their lack of incidents. It would be reassuring to assume that this demonstrated aircraft were becoming far more reliable than previously with pilots more ably equipped for the task, yet it also would be prudent to accept that documentary evidence may not have been as rigorous as it could have been.

A significant and fatal event took place in the summer of 1913 which brought the location of the air station at Dysart Farm to an end. A routine flight in progress with pilot Lt Desmond L. Arthur, in his BE 2, went horribly wrong causing the aircraft to spiral out of control, throwing Lt Arthur out of the cockpit to his death. His plane crashed a few hundred yards further away near the beach at Lunan Bay. An investigation into the cause of the fatal accident took place by the Royal Aero Club where they found the right-hand wing had been repaired following previous breakage. Their conclusion was that the repair had been poorly completed and had been covered over. The individual responsible was never identified. The report to this effect recommended that *'future repairs be checked by experienced inspectors and logged on the aircraft's dossier'*. There had been several debatable reports relating to this incident over the subsequent years which raised questions on many aspects of safety. This horrific accident, however, was not the last heard of Lt Arthur.

B.E.2 - Early production - Wikimedia Commons/Public Domain

Major Burke then considered the topography of the land at Dysart as being an unsuitable area for use as an air station. Following a further investigation, he found the Broomfield site, north of the town of Montrose. Situated close to the Aberdeen- London railway, with a helpful prevailing wind from the links., this location would be perfect. Following the completion of three Indian Army sheds which were built in a crescent formation in December 1913, specifically erected to house aircraft, the air station moved to its new site in early 1914.

To assist with navigation and sighting of the airfield by pilots, these early aircraft '*sheds*', were decorated in a striped pattern which could be spotted from a distance. The haar rolling in from the North Sea could often be brutal in its attack, rapidly blotting out vantage points. In these early days of powered flight with no navigational instrumentation other than visual recognition of the terrain, the candy stripes were often a welcome sight for the inexperienced airmen.

Early aircraft outside 'Burkes Sheds' circa 1914 – photograph courtesy of Montrose Air Station and Heritage Centre

Striped Burke's Sheds at Montrose circa 1914 – Photograph courtesy Montrose Air Station

Heritage Centre

These sheds are in excellent condition today, registered as 'Class A' listed buildings and fondly known as '*Major Burkes*' Sheds. These three buildings, which sit adjacent to the Montrose Air Station Heritage Centre, are the best examples of early aircraft hangars and hold international significance.

Events in Europe were now becoming universally strained and the likelihood of war was approaching by early 1914. The Broomfield site was now suitably established and reconnaissance missions continued well into June of that year.

At the outbreak of war, in August 1914, Major Burke led No 2 Squadron, one of the first units to fly out to France. His course took him to Dover then across the English Channel. He recorded in his diaries that he was not '*best pleased* 'to see one of his junior officers landed before him.'

Lieutenant H.D. Harvey-Kelly had flown directly overland to Amiens rather than follow the coastal route taken by the squadron. Burke wrote in his diary, '*As I was approaching Amiens, I saw an aircraft already on the ground. It was Harvey-Kelly, and becoming famous as the first British pilot to land in France was worth the reprimand.*'

Replica of Harvey-Kelly's BE2 built by Alan Doe and team at Montrose Air Station Heritage Centre – Writer's own photograph - 2019

Training of these pilots became the responsibility of one notable figure who was also one of the pioneers of army flying having attained his flying certificate in 1912 – Major Francis Fitzgerald Waldron. He joined the RFC in January 1913 and became a flying instructor in October 1914, before becoming Squadron Commander in 1915.

The RFC suffered horrendous casualties during WWI, with many being lost in training as well as in action. Sergeant Mack, an American serviceman stationed at Montrose in early 1918 is recorded as stating *'there's a crash every day and a funeral every week.'*

Situated between mountains, the Angus Glens and the sea, with the menacing haar rolling in on the tide without warning, sometimes eradicated all vision of the landing site. There would have been no doubt about the extreme challenges for pilots.

During the WWI years, Montrose Air Station was a busy military installation with many aircraft now flying missions from there, primarily with Sopwith Pups; Sopwith Camels; Longhorns; Bristol Scouts; Avros and B.E.2s. It is reported that during the WWI period, Montrose received additional four squadrons, *'No 25 in September 1915, No 43 in April 1916, No 83 in January 1917 and No 80 as a fighter squadron in November of the same year'*

Various new aircraft were also accepted and as the air station expanded, the need for additional technical buildings, including hangars was recognised. The War Department valued the location and the efforts made by the valiant aircrew; it therefore authorised the building of suitable accommodation for trainee pilots and their instructors plus the addition of a further three hangars.

The importance which the air station held required the necessity for supplementary sites to be made available and by 1918, Edzell had become a satellite air station for Montrose whilst Auldbar, situated between Forfar and Montrose, became a satellite airship mooring site, for RAF Longside air station at Peterhead in Aberdeenshire.

Throughout the WWI years, Montrose hosted many overseas visitors including No 82 and No 85 Canadian Reserve Squadrons in January 1917. After the Armistice, Montrose continued as a training school for pilots until 1920.

Major Burke was not lucky enough - he died in action on the 9th April 1917. He is commemorated at St Mary's Cathedral in Limerick, Ireland as *'Lieutenant Colonel Charles James Burke DSO, Soldier, Pilot,*

Commanding Officer, Military Aviation Visionary and Pioneer.'

Major Waldron also served with distinction but was also killed in action on 3rd July 1916. He is honoured by the bridge crossing the railway line at Montrose Air Station being named after him – *'Waldron's Bridge.'* These two great soldiers will be remembered as founder members of the RFC, where soldiers were airmen in advance of the formation of the Royal Air Force.

Burke and Waldron at Montrose – photograph courtesy of Montrose Air Station Heritage

Centre

During the 'Expansion Period', the RAF saw some economies of scale both in its workforce and air stations, with many of the wartime airfields closing. There was a shift to civil aviation, which was tardy at first in

Scotland, until it was realised that the islands could be serviced via air. Some civilian staff were employed for maintenance purposes at Montrose and 'Major Burke's sheds' were once again put to good use by being an area for machine gun repair and preservation. Montrose stayed quiet, patiently waiting for a time when its service was once again required.

The peaceful *'between the war years period'* didn't last too long. The 1930's saw the swift and sudden rise of power of Germany's Nazi Party led by its dictator, Adolph Hitler, who raised a new threat by increasing his vast military resources and utilised terrifying tactics in the eastern European states. Britain was bracing itself for another bloody conflict and plans were made to reinforce the military resources it would require to meet the challenges that it was about to face. Scottish airfields were again designated as practical sites for training units, though many had to be hastily built with temporary buildings. RAF Montrose, however, was ready! Its Somerfield track runways, concrete perimeter tracks and hangars were already in situ – its defences had been maintained and with minimal effort was in an operational state to resume active service.

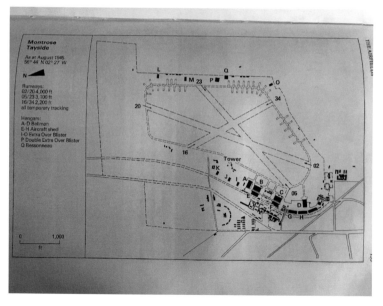

Montrose Airfield – courtesy of Montrose Air Station Heritage Centre

This time, Montrose would now take on the role as a *Flying Training*

31

Command Station training novice pilots to earn their *'wings'*. In 1936, No 8 Service Flying Training School was in place, with the aim to give 3 months flying to 48 trainees followed by 3 months of advanced instruction by which time they should have the ability to join RAF squadrons as fully qualified service pilots. The types of aircraft now had radically changed with the Air Station now dealing with Anson; Oxford; Hart Trainers; Tiger Moth; Masters; Hawker Audaxes with the numbers and different types anticipated to increase in numbers. Set to face another major international conflict, almost 21 years having passed since *'the war to end all wars,'* however, this would be a very different type of warfare.

The technical buildings required for the increase in personnel and activity were rapidly installed and the defences were strengthened not only on site but in the surrounding vicinity. Tank traps were laid along the beaches supported by pillboxes to deter any seaward landing from enemy raiders. Air raid shelters and Battle Headquarters were developed with a myriad of temporary *'huts and hangars'* made available to meet the needs of the service.

The Flying School at Montrose, was renamed as the *Special Flying Training School* (SFTS) with aircraft now numbering forty-four Oxfords and thirty-one Harts. Masters soon arrived to supplement the total which had increased to 100 aircraft. Two Anson squadrons also were temporarily based at Montrose during this time. The Flying Training School continued to grow with aircraft and personnel arriving from RAF Drem at East Lothian. This was an extremely busy School for new pilots and as such had now two satellites; Stracathro from June 1940 then Edzell by July.

Training during wartime conditions introduced new dangers especially on night flying, especially as enemy aircraft could be advancing from off shore. Night flight training in aircraft with no radio control in a blackout with only tiny *'goose neck flares'* as a guide, easily lost to view, proved more than a challenge for some of these brave young men. With the North Sea on one side and the Grampian mountains at the other it was not a task for the fainthearted. To protect the airfield from enemy marauders, fighter squadrons were also stationed at Montrose which could be scrambled in minutes and take off in any direction. Another hazard for

32

the nervous trainees to cope with.

A number of fighter squadrons also sent detachments to Montrose late 1939-1940 with some longer periods of fighter attachment when the Hurricanes of 232 Squadron moved from Elgin, before finally moving to Abbotsinch.

Montrose lying right on the coast and being situated on the main rail link between London and Aberdeen, lay vulnerable to attack and following the first air raid on British mainland on naval units in the Firth of Forth on the 16th October 1939, improvements to the airfield defences were made by building pillboxes at strategic points along the boundary. Pickett-Hamilton Forts were also built into the runway as a means of defence especially against any attempt of an airborne landing.

The Pickett-Hamilton retractable fort was an innovative idea, placed on the landing area flush with the ground with the ability to bear a 7- ton weight should an aircraft taxi over it. In the event of an attack, they could be raised three feet above ground swiftly either by compressed air or hydraulics. Each one could contain two men with weapons who would keep look out and raise the fort when an attack was imminent.

Hamilton Pickett Fort at Montrose Air Station- photograph courtesy of M Craib

33

Fort at Montrose mechanism flooded - Photograph courtesy of M Craib

Tank traps were laid on the beaches and pillbox sentries guarded the area close to the perimeter track of the airfield.

When the Germans invaded and occupied Denmark and Norway, the situation changed dramatically, with access to the Scottish coast now more manageable. Air activity over and close to the north-east coast then increased with aircraft losses on both sides occurring.

Local resident, Sandy Donald writes in an Angus Writers Anthology, recollecting *'some spectacular manoeuvres being carried out by the Allies. Aeroplanes zoomed over the Basin and stunted in the area of the beach and golf course.'*

The Basin alludes to Montrose Basin – a tidal estuary and sanctuary for wildlife

He also remembers seeing *'a convoy of ships heading north about six miles out. They were protected by Barrage Balloons and a Sunderland flying boat was circling around them.'*

RAF Montrose was bombed on the 18th July 1940 by a single marauder causing eleven casualties, two of which were fatal and damaged 13 aircraft. The problem lay in that they flew in low under the radar, being unable to be detected early enough to raise an alarm.

Montrose was attacked again on Friday 25th October by German raiders appearing suddenly, again flying low over the sea, thus giving that vital element of surprise. The town was bombed first, hitting a factory, patrol and fishing boats at the docks. Other bombs landed on the golf course, some nearby cottages and the beaches at Ferryden and Rossie Island, where some of them landed unexploded. RAF Montrose experienced significant damage which could have been catastrophic as also three of the bombs remained unexploded. The cost however, was still considerable with numerous casualties following the raid, some loss of life and damage to a substantial number of aircraft and buildings.

The records from 'Fighter Command – Report for 25th October 1940 Attack, on Area Montrose to St Andrews 18.30-1900 hours states:

'*2 raids totalling about 10 aircraft appeared 25 miles east of Montrose made landfall north of the Tay. 2 attacks were made on the RAF station at Montrose by 3 He 111s flying from E to W and diving to about100 feet, dropping sticks of bombs and firing machine guns.*'

A few minutes later the fishing town of Arbroath was next to feel the German fury with the RNAS base, HMS Condor being the objective.

The No 2 Flying Instructors Training School started in January 1942 and continued instruction took place throughout this period. The RAF recognised that '*experienced pilots did not automatically become good instructors without specific training for the role*'. From 1942, instructors for Flying Training Schools. Operational Training Units and the new Advanced Training Units, were taught at Montrose. The' *Link Trainer*' a primitive but effective early form of flight simulator, affectionately known as '*the Blue Box*' played a major role in the training programme for pilots. It offered the opportunity to supplement airborne flight training by simulating different scenarios by which the student could practice in the relative safety of the air station.

Link Trainer based at Montrose Air Station Heritage Centre – Photograph Writer's own - 2019

These Flying Instructors were the silent heroes of WWII. A previous student at Montrose, who gained his wings there and demonstrated *'above average'* abilities was Pilot Officer Gordon Levett who declared *'it was rotten luck to become a flying instructor. That it almost certainly saved my life was no consolation. Like my comrades, I wanted to risk my life, not save it. Becoming an instructor was to most young pilots, a fate worse than the possibility of being killed in action'*

The notion that being an instructor was a *'risk-free'* occupation was in fact far from the truth. Instructors flew more hours than any of the service operational pilots did, also they had to be versatile and flexible enough to fly a variety of different types of aircraft at any given time, and in any adverse condition. Experience did not guarantee survival!

Fighter and reconnaissance Squadrons, and the Air Sea Rescue Craft Unit, also operated during this time and continued until almost the end of the wartime activities.

When the war in Europe was eventually over, the RAF were left with a surplus of qualified pilots. No 2 Flying Instructors School was disbanded. RAF Montrose's association with training pilots for war had finally come to an end. In the post-war period, RAF Montrose used the satellite for No 44 Maintenance Unit at Edzell for aircraft storage and from 24 March 1947 to 31 March 1950 was home to No 63 Maintenance Unit operating as a repair and salvage unit.

RAF Montrose however, played a major position with the Mountain Rescue Service which was established in 1944 and originated in Wales. The Montrose Mountain Rescue Team was one of the first of ten bases with regular training exercises which were carried out in the Angus Glens and surrounding countryside. With the closure of the Air Station in 1950, the team moved to RAF Edzell and eventually to RAF Leuchars near St Andrews in 1955.

When the RAF finally vacated the Air Station, it was used occasionally by British Airways helicopters for night training in 1977-1978 and by RAF Hercules for tactical exercises in October of that year.

The one-time military facility is now managed as the Montrose Air Station Heritage Centre, a fully accredited museum, which exists to tell the story of the brave men who risked their lives for their country, through two World Wars in order that we today, as a nation, can once more live at peace.

MONTROSE AIR STATION HERITAGE CENTRE

The air station at Montrose has seen the efforts from courageous young pilots over two World Wars, yet still survives today as a fully functioning and highly successful Heritage Centre which attracts global interest from aviation enthusiasts of all ages. It has retained some of its wartime buildings, which look as they did during the wars.

Like many war time establishments tragedies frequently occurred to affect the lives of many young men and women. The risk of losing a friend, a colleague or a spouse was very real and happened all too often. RAF Montrose was no exception. There were many happy times when friendships were struck, romances bloomed and firm team bonding occurred. This was an environment that even through the horrors of

37

warfare, the station personnel formed close networks and supported each other in times of trauma, death and destruction. Like many disused military bases around Britain, memories and extrasensory perceptions can still linger in the atmosphere and in areas where activity was continually fraught with tension. Time passes so swiftly for us all. Today, few remain to share their wartime experiences yet we are fortunate to have the benefit of media technology and publications to keep remembrances alive to ensure none will forget that history is our past.

The three sheds built in 1913 to house the military aircraft remain in situ at the air station. First used in action from January 1st 1914, they are excellent specimens of the oldest accommodation for housing military aircraft being in exceptional condition and considered to be a rare find within the British Isles.

Initially the old wooden headquarters and surrounding buildings were left just as they were used following the last days of action in WWII. Over the following years, some of the surrounding land area of the site and the Bellman hangars were then taken over for industrial use, like many sites over the country. Subsequently, a dedicated group of local volunteers and enthusiasts saw the potential for the restoration of the air station, back to the days of its former purpose and so, the Montrose Aerodrome Museum Society was formed in April 1983. These intrepid volunteers with the aid of donations, charitable contributions and a significant amount of faithful commitment, transformed the headquarters into an exhibition centre complete with authentic artefacts, audio-visual and interactive displays.

The new buildings house WWI replica B.E.2 and Sopwith Camel aircraft painstakingly built to exact specifications by Alan Doe and many of the volunteers who have specialist engineering backgrounds complete with a passion for the task, combined with a total commitment to the success of the airfield's museum.

A feature of the fascinating exhibits is a replica of the Spitfire Mk VB in the markings of 602 (City of Glasgow) Squadron, which was purchased by contributions of people living in Arbroath and surrounding areas at the time of the hostilities. The 'Red Lichtie' takes pride of place in front of the Commanding Officer's office and headquarters exhibition building.

Montrose is like no other usual aircraft museum as it has its own permanent 'residents' who can make themselves known at the most unlikely of times and holds 'a mystery which creates more questions than answers'. These premises have seen life and death over two of the most noxious periods of British History and it is understood some of these brave airmen who lost their lives, still 'reside' in the atmospheric conditions.

There is however, a presence which has attached itself to the Air Station Heritage Centre and many would say, '*is still lingering from those tortured war time years and has a reluctance to move on*'. Unexplained happenings and visual manifestations relating to events and Heritage Centre personnel have been recounted on many occasions and by many visitors to the area. Specialist paranormal investigative teams have conducted research studies, television studios have produced documentaries and there have been many fine books produced about the ghostly manifestations and unexplained activity there.

The unusual occurrences first started following the untimely death of Lt. Desmond Arthur in 1913, where it was indicated a poor repair caused his accident. Sometime later, a further investigation concluded that Lt Arthur had *been 'stunt flying'* and had been the sole cause of the accident. It was after this declaration, strange and unexplainable sightings and phenomena presented, almost as though the deceased was furious about the decision. Much later, the incident was re-investigated and finally Lt Arthur was absolved from any blame attributed to the loss of his life.

Ever since that time there have been sightings of airmen seen in the buildings or out in the airfield itself, aviators wearing flying suits disappearing into walls and even aircraft disappearing over the airfield. These supernatural occurrences have taken place through WWI and WWII years and still are prevalent today having been seen by volunteer personnel who work in the centre.

Visitors to the Montrose Air Station Heritage Centre are always fascinated when they are advised about the *'Montrose Ghost'* as it is commonly known, but it would appear likely to be more than one, indeed probably many, mysterious and unexplained forces at work in that area.

Lt. Desmond Arthur – photograph courtesy of Montrose Air Station Heritage Centre

Unexplained appearances of airmen dressed in WWI flying suits and goggles were prevalent during the wartime era of the 'forties' as well as the visual detections of WWI and WWII fighter aircraft from the base seen by many individuals around Montrose. Footsteps, voices and ghostly figures have been seen on many occasions. Apparition appearances have taken place now over the decades making Montrose Air Station one of the most haunted sites in the country. When the haar rolls in on the tide from the North Sea, the air station takes on an eerie atmosphere and a sense of unreality. Personal experiences of encountering WWI and WWII airmen, distinguishable by their flying gear faced by volunteer members of the Heritage Centre are recounted on guided tours which adds to the mystery of their visit. Forbes Inglis, a local historian and author who holds a special interest in the paranormal, details many instances in his publication where he has experienced strange phenomena during his time working as a Development Officer at Montrose.

The most significant spectre of all, Lieutenant Desmond Arthur was heralded in a drama production held at the Air Station to celebrate the centenary of RFC Montrose with the guest of honour being His Royal Highness Prince Edward. Acclaimed playwright, Elizabeth Doe, the wife of Alan Doe, Chairman 2001-2017, who was instrumental in building the replica B.E.2, delighted the packed audience with her poignant dialogue between Desmond and Major Burke.

In conclusion, Montrose Air Station holds the undisputed distinction for being one of the most haunted air stations in the country.

The county of Angus is blessed having a facility like the Montrose Air Station Heritage Centre where the memories of those brave men and women will always be with us and will be there well into the future for our children and grandchildren to learn.

HERITAGE SITE CONTACT DETAILS

Montrose Air Station Heritage Centre

Waldron Road

Broomfield

Montrose

Angus

DD10 9BD

01674 678222

rafmontrose.org.uk

National Museum of Flight

East Fortune Airfield

North Berwick

EH395 5LF

0300 1236789

Dumfries and Galloway Aviation Museum

Former Control Tower

Heathhall Industrial Estate

Dumfries

DG1 3PH

01387 251623

Dundee Museum of Transport - As at June 2021

Unit 10 - Market Mews

Market Street

Dundee

DD13LA

01382 455196

info@ dmoft.co.uk

CHAPTER 5
RNAS ARBROATH - HMS CONDOR

Fleet Air Arm - Training

56°34'46.50 N 2°27'36.52 W

The threat of war and enemy invasion indicated an urgent need for additional sites for military training to be made available. In April 1939, The Admiralty announced their decision to build another air station on the north-east coast and construction work started thereafter on agricultural land just north of the fishing town of Arbroath which is roughly the halfway point between RAF Montrose and the port of Dundee. The Air Station took fourteen months to complete and was operational from the 19th June 1940. The area was ideally situated adjacent to the main London-Aberdeen railway line and near to Colliston Station, (now demolished). RNAS Arbroath, commissioned as HMS Condor, was a Fleet Air Arm base primarily used for training.

Arbroath Air Station is the fourth ship to bear the name 'HMS Condor'. The first was a gun vessel of 780 tons, built in 1876, who saw service in Alexandria and action in the Sudan in 1885. The second was a steel sloop of 980 tons commissioned in 1900, intended to serve in the Pacific but unfortunately sank with *all hands,* on 3rd December 1901. A tanker of 227 tons was the third ship which was commissioned for patrol service in 1914, but was wrecked in the same year.

With four main tarmac surfaced runways, a purpose-built *aircraft carrier* sized landing area was constructed on the airfield used for training aircrew in deck landing operations. A similar facility was constructed later, a few miles south on the coast at East Haven (HMS Peewit).

Hangars, Bellman type, were situated around the perimeter with a reserve Bellman hangar closer to Colliston – just in case Condor aircraft were put out of action in an enemy attack.

Bellman Hangar at Perimeter of RM Condor – Photograph Writers own taken 2019 – (demolished in 2021)

During WWII, Arbroath was one of the Royal Navy's busiest Air Stations with No2 Observers School, Deck Landing Training (DLT) and a Naval Air Signals School all operating from this site. The main observer units flew a variety of aircraft including: Swordfish, Albacores, Walrus, Fulmars, Sharks, Proctors and Barracuda with squadrons consisting of up to twenty- five aircraft at that time.

The war -time task of training Observers at HMS Condor was Part II of the programme, having taken it over from RNAS Yeovilton. Part I was completed at RNAS Ford first, with the training having taken twenty-two months to complete in total.

Fairey Albacores on deck landing training ready for take-off at HMS Condor - RN Official Photograph A 19574 IWM - Wikimedia Commons/Public Domain

It was one of these aircraft listed which was involved in a local incident whereby the aircraft glided down a street in Arbroath after the pilot bailed out and came to a stop, suspended between two houses leaving scrape marks on buildings, which were still visible until recently.

There were various other types of training undertaken at HMS Condor during WWII, which made Arbroath an extremely busy site with both day and night flying, (TAG) – Telegraphist Air Gunner training; Radar Training; Torpedo Attack Training, Target Towing; and Service Trials – which evaluated aircraft, weapons and equipment.

With the German occupation of Norway and the threat of invasion considered to be increasingly possible, airfields on the east coast became a prime target for enemy attack. There were sporadic raids ongoing, but when airbases at Aalborg in northern Denmark and Stavanger in Norway brought the enemy aircraft much closer to the north-east Scottish coast, air activity increased accordingly. When the last allied troops left Norwegian territory in June 1940, there was the rapid German *blitzkrieg*, which commenced throughout northern Europe. The fall of France and the Dunkirk evacuation meant dark times for the British, which culminated with the Battle of Britain between July and October.

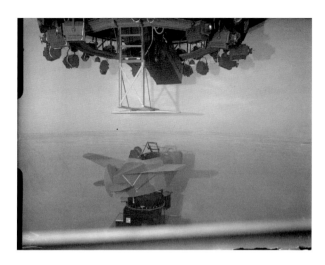

The Torpedo Attack Trainer at Arbroath - SJ Beadell RN Photographer A18248 IWM - Wikimedia Commons/Public Domain

Defence of these installations were in the remit of Army detachments with initially a few firearms only available. Winston Churchill, Prime Minister from 1940, declared,

'It must be understood by all ranks that they are expected to fight and die in the defence of these airfields........ every airfield should be a stronghold of fighting air ground men and not the abode of uniformed civilians.

The *Purdah* Scheme enabled any airfield under attack to radio for assistance to a central control using a coded call sign detailing the enemy strength, parachutists etc and Army units could be hastily moved to the scene. Pillboxes were speedily erected at strategic points around the perimeter with smaller machine gun posts protecting the landing areas.

At Arbroath on the edge of the runway, the concrete base is all that remains of an Alan-Williams Turret. This form of defence had a steel dome shaped cover which was set above a steel and brick lined pit which could be rotated 360°on rollers to allow firing access by a Lewis gun either through the door or through a circular roof opening.

There was space inside for at least two men with folding steel seating – one to be the gunner and the other to rotate the steel dome. There were 199 ordered during WWII at a cost of £125 each, with only a few remaining which generally can be found on the edges of old disused airfields in the United Kingdom.

Concrete remains of airfield defence at HMS Condor -Pickett-Hamilton retractable fort - photo courtesy of M Craib

It is hard to imagine these beautiful areas in a state of war, and although the beaches have been swept for mines and cleared over time, and until fairly recently, there was still the occasion where an explosive device had been found on the dunes or washed up on the tide, still live after decades since the last armistice.

HMS Condor, like the majority of all RNAS stations, was built to the same standard by RM Engineers, none more so than the impressive control tower which stands majestically at the side of the runway.

The standard design comprises a ground floor plan with three different heights of towers each designed to suit the needs of the station. Arbroath has a 4-storey control tower and is fairly unique as it is a *Category C Listed Building* and is one of two surviving examples of this particular type of tower which features an ambulance and crash tender garage. Listed in May 2006, is noted by Historic Environment Scotland as being *'important in terms of naval and WWII history as well as local significance.'*

On the evening of 25th October 1940 following the air attack on Montrose, which is situated about 14 miles away, Arbroath was the next target for the German bombers. Information obtained from HMS Condor states,

'at 18.45 the station was attacked by enemy aircraft. An estimated 12 bombs and 100 incendiaries were dropped from two Heinkel 111s and 1 Dornier. Of the bombs dropped, two failed to explode and four only partially exploded. A squadron office was demolished and two other buildings had their roofs blown off. Otherwise, the station air defence consisted chiefly of Lewis guns manned by the Army, who unfortunately thinking that the enemy aircraft were friendly and about to land, did not

fire a single shot until it was too late.'

There is also a personal recollection from Dr David Balfour who was only seven years old at the time of the attack but could remember his father who worked in the aircraft stores at HMS Condor recall an incident as follows:

'On the following morning the traffic to Arbroath town was diverted because a mine was dangling from a parachute trapped in a tree at the roadside about quarter of a mile north-west of the main entrance to the camp. Ropes and a block and tackle were required for the engineers to defuse and then remove the mine. There was a great relief that the mine did not explode.'

Dr Balfour's sister was cycling past the airfield on the main road that evening. He reported that *'she saw the German aircraft flying towards her. The explosions prompted her to jump off her cycle into the roadside ditch. She believed the aircraft was firing machine-guns and she clearly identified the German insignia on the wings as it flew over. She thought it was a Heinkel 111.'*

Reports indicate the attack was from a very low-level approach and the mine would have been dropped from a much greater height. It would appear the air station received little damage with no loss of life but still had damage to property and injuries to two individuals.

By the end of 1941, three air firing ranges were in progress, at Lunan Bay, at a position close to Stonehaven and also close to Arbroath. Due to incidents involving near misses at Arbroath, the first two were used until 1943.

The Signals School started in 1942 and the RNAS station was also used as a base for aircrew during *rest* sessions. At this time a new system of centralised maintenance was started. This entailed the heavy maintenance and repairs on aircraft being performed by a single unit at each station. (Previously this had been done by individual squadrons.) The use of Dutch Barns to house the aircraft in, lying around various sites past the perimeter, was intended to minimise potential damage from any further air attacks.

Dutch Barn at Perimeter of RM Condor – photograph Writers own taken 2019 – (demolished in 2021)

Old Water Tank beside Bellman Hangar at Colliston - photograph courtesy M Craib - (demolished in 2021)

During 1942-43, flying training continued in addition to those mentioned already, there were also Lysanders; Hurricanes and Skuas but as the war was drawing to a close in 1944, the departure of the Observers School and many squadrons took place although bombing practice still continued.

By the end of 1945 the air station's operational flying days ended with the coming of the jet-age and HMS Condor took on a new role of technical and new- entry training with the main body of apprentices

50

joining in January 1946. Eventually there were 1500 trainees, with HMS Condor leading the role for total training of the Fleet Air Arm mechanical branch during 1946-1949.

In 1961, the freedom of the burgh was bestowed on HMS Condor but in 1967, the station was finally closed as an RNAS site and its future was in the balance for a period of two years.

Short Skyvan - used for parachute training - Wikimedia Commons/Public Domain

The airfield continued under naval control and by the late 1960s the authorities agreed the station would be an ideal location for a commando unit of the Royal Marines who could use the surrounding countryside for their mountain and Arctic training. 45 Commando, Royal Marines, moved into the station in 1970 and remain in residence at the site. Condor's flying days are not over yet, as the unit has its own helicopter flight and parachute training from a Skyvan continues.

Today, the base is named RM Condor and continues fully operational with its personnel participating in NATO and other significant military exercises. It has an artificial ski slope on site for Arctic warfare practice, has a CBNR specialised group base as well as 45 Commando and is one of the most important military sites in Scotland.

Extensive construction on the RM Condor site car park in June 1995, uncovered three wartime propellers, sadly in a poor state of repair. Once cleaned up, the task of identification took place with the assistance of the Fleet Air Arm Museum.

They identified the first to be an American variable pitch propeller likely fitted to a Grumman Hellcat or Corsair which were in use during WWII by the Fleet Air Arm. The second was a British variable pitch propeller, which could have been fitted to a variety of aircraft such as Hawker Sea Hurricane, Fairey Albacore or Blackburn Skua. The third was unable to be identified due to its poor condition.

The American propeller was restored and following completion of the New Headquarters for Comacchio Group building, was placed on display outside the main building.

WWII Propeller excavated at RM Condor - photograph courtesy of RM Condor Arbroath

On a recent visit to RM Condor, I was presented with historical details relating to the base during WWII and the period thereafter and for readers who may be interested, the following is a breakdown of functions carried out on the base.

52

HMS CONDOR

Commissioned	19th June 1940
Deck Landing Training	June 1940 –April 1943
Swordfish/Albacore	October 1940 – February 1941
TAG Training	October 1940 – February 1941
Observer Training	March 1941 – March 1945
RADAR Training	January 1941 – May 1947
Target Towing	October 1940 – December 1944
Trials Squadron	August 1940 – March 1943
Air Engineering School – Sea Otter	December 1946 – October 1949
Ansons	
Firefly	
Sea Hornet	1948
45 Commando RM – arrived from Stonehouse	1970
Comacchio Group RM – Company formed	May 1980

CHAPTER 6 – RNAS EAST HAVEN – HMS PEEWIT

Flying Training Command – Flying Instructors School

56°43'48° N 2°27'05°W

The village of East Haven is situated only a few miles south of Arbroath and is surrounded by flat agricultural land. The Fleet Air Arm, the branch of the Royal Navy responsible for the operation of naval aircraft, required additional sites to train its naval pilots, given the vulnerability of the country. As the war gathered momentum, aircrew training units increased rapidly in size and as Arbroath was already at capacity, the Admiralty made the decision to seek a suitable site for an additional airfield close by. The land geography at East Haven was perfect for the task and by November 1941, the build commenced with the runways and hangars, of which there were twenty-four dispersed around the airfield perimeter. Two camps for accommodation were also built nearby at Scryne and Sparrowmuir.

At first the air station was commissioned as HMS Dotterel on the 1st May 1943, then a few days later was changed to HMS Peewit. This was to remain in line with all Naval Air Stations classed as *land locked ships* being allotted the name of birds. It had the usual format of Royal Naval four runway tarmac system with a perimeter track, one of which was marked outwith paint as a deck landing site. It had the distinction of having a dummy carrier island – '*HMS Spurious*, for *realistic deck landing and control training purposes.* This was a 1930's Albion bus which had been converted to resemble the island of an aircraft carrier.

The complexities of landing an aircraft on a carrier required a Deck Landing Control Officer (DLCO) who was given the nickname *Batsman.* These officers were experienced aircraft pilots who used high visibility paddles, similar in design to table tennis bats, in order to signal instructions to the aircraft pilots as they prepared to land on a carrier. To become a *Batsman* a pilot had to train at East Haven for a period of three weeks. At first, this task was only reserved for the more advanced pilots but as the war progressed, the need for experienced pilots for this role diminished and more junior officers were trained for the role. A further duty the DLCO's performed was to lead the handling of aircraft on the deck, which included the spreading and folding of wings, the removal of damaged aircraft and the management of fires should they occur on deck.

HMS Spurious' the dummy aircraft carrier deck island on the runway at Easthaven - RN Official photograph IWN - Wikimedia Commons/Public Domain

There is one thing that can be said about the British in times of crisis – they know how to adapt!

Easily transportable, HMS Spurious was used at HMS Condor and HMS Peewit, as both sites were used for deck landing training purposes. The runways were painted out as aircraft carrier landing sites giving the novice pilots an opportunity to practice the short, narrow landing space. Today there is no evidence left of the deck paint, but hardly surprising after this length of time.

Deck Landing at HMS Peewit with HMS Spurious just visible at bottom left of photograph - Photograph courtesy of R Woomble/Fleet Air Arm Museum Yeovilton

A RNAS four storey control tower of similar design at nearby HMS Condor was in place overseeing the runways, but now sadly has been demolished in the post war period.

The accommodation was sufficient to house up to four squadrons which eased the serious overcrowding conditions at Arbroath. The Deck Landing Training School was transferred to HMS Peewit from HMS Condor in November 1943 and operated a variety of aircraft types, including Sea Hurricanes and Barracudas. Fairey Swordfish aircraft, nicknamed *stringbags* were used to introduce pilots to the use of the arrester wire, before moving onto faster and more powerful types of planes.

The ground or *shipside* of the operations was 731 Squadron which was formed specifically for the training of Deck Landing Control Officers in December 1943. Now this was an art form indeed where precision and attention to detail was required, to ensure the safe storage of aircraft on the flight deck.

East Haven also became the site for aircrew training in torpedo attack bombing, using targets in the nearby inshore waters, which required Swordfish and Barracuda aircraft and they were used until 1945, thereafter American built Avengers were based there for the task.

There was still capacity on site to take a further two non-flying units, the Aircraft Handling Flight and Fire Fighting School which were housed there until there was accommodation released back in Arbroath by late 1945. In the early post war period, the requirements for the air station began to reduce, but the deck landing and torpedo bombing training continued until the last training aircraft left on the 15th July 1946.

HMS Peewit's last inhabitants were personnel from the Operational Flying School and the air station finally closed in August 1946, being placed then on the Care and Maintenance schedule from Arbroath. Local farmers then resumed the use of the site from 1949.

Some of the hangars and the remains of old brick buildings still survive but the land mostly went back to the use of agriculture. Some sections of the runways were still used post war for parachute drops as they were still in a reasonable condition. The Commando Unit based at Arbroath used the facility infrequently thereafter, for exercises involving helicopters. The brick- built Battle Command Headquarters, which was set back from the runways and perimeter tracks, was demolished at the end of the twentieth century due to substantial deterioration. Strange to think that this building at one time was a busy operational place of safety, then was slowly left to decay over the decades, ending as a significant hazard, labelled for demolition.

Hatton Brick Post – photograph -courtesy of R Woomble

Hatton House Grounds - courtesy of R Woomble

Hangar at Hatton Farm - photograph courtesy of R Woomble

Some of the hangars, however, are still visible from the roadside at nearby Hatton Farm and are in remarkable condition given the timespan since their previous use. Some surviving military buildings can also be seen in the grounds and around Hatton House, however most are now in a derelict state, but one can easily imagine this site being alive with personnel and aircraft activity, all playing a crucial role in the defence of our nation.

Demolition of Command Bunker – photograph courtesy of R Woomble

CHAPTER 7 - RAF KINNELL

Flying Training Command – Flying Instructors School – Satellite

56°38'29.72 N 2°38'51.80 W

The small hamlet of Kinnell sits amidst agricultural land about 1 mile from the village of Friockheim in Angus. With its largely flat landscape situated close to Arbroath, Edzell, Stracathro and only a few miles south of Montrose, it made an excellent choice for placing a small wartime airfield, with its primary function being a site for training pilots in preparation for operational duties.

Approval for land acquisition was obtained in March 1941 for the construction for an airfield to be used as a satellite for RAF Tealing, situated approximately three miles north of the city of Dundee. Some hedges were removed from boundary fields to create a V-shaped runway system and work commenced to provide the necessary technical buildings and other accommodation that was required for a small wartime site.

The main technical buildings were of temporary huts with Blister hangars in the dispersal areas and on other outlying parts of the airfield. The communal sites were situated just north-east of the airfield with the WAAF site a little further back from the main buildings.

Watch/Control Tower at RAF Kinnell - photograph Writer's Own taken 2019

The runways were of asphalt and are still visible today, although a road now cuts through them from Kinnell to the Forfar - Montrose road junction. Remains of the watch tower which is an unusual type, is located adjacent to the runway system, also there is residual evidence of wartime brick-built structures that sadly, are now in a derelict state.

When No 56 Operational Training Unit moved to Tealing in March 1942 with their Hurricanes and Masters aircraft, it immediately started using Kinnell as its satellite. The first aircraft to be housed at Kinnell were four Lysanders from the OTU target-towing Flight. From 16th September 1942, night flying training was started with *circuits and bumps.*

Brick built Guard Post at Kinnell – photograph Writer's own taken 2019

The remit of the OTU was to train fighter pilots advanced from their elementary flying training and to progress them onto being operational pilots ready for posting to awaiting squadrons. Many of the instructors held an operational role in emergency situations as they were also affiliated to the Peterhead sector, north of Aberdeen, as No 556 Squadron. Their remit was to conduct convoy patrols up the north east coastline and escorts for sea-going vessels. The first scramble from Kinnell took place on 6th April 1943, with two aircraft shadowing a convoy, until relieved by aircraft from Peterhead. This was a regular occurrence which provided some very useful operational flying experience for the more advanced trainees.

The OTU was renamed as No 1 Combat Training Wing in October 1943 specialising in *air-firing and evasive action* with each pilot having a requirement to also complete five hours night flying at Kinnell.

Firing Butts at Kinnell Airfield - photograph – Writer's own taken 2019

Again, the Unit was renamed in January 1944 as the No1 Tactical Exercise Unit with Kinnell remaining as the satellite station. The remit was similar as before, except fighter-bomber training was an additional competency, as was expected at that time for fighter squadrons, with Spitfires joining the Hurricanes on site. The air station continued these operational duties until the TEU was disbanded in July 1944.

The airfield was then taken over by No2 Flying Instructors School at Montrose, as a base for its 'G' Flight from September of that year, flying Oxfords and Masters aircraft as an advanced training unit until July 1945.

After their departure, the airfield was used as a Maintenance Unit, allocated to No 44 MU based at Edzell air station for aircraft storage. The site was also used by No 260 MU based at Errol, Perthshire. That service continued until the air station eventually closed in December 1947.

Kinnell, like many of the unused wartime airfields that lay dormant in the post war years, came to life during the 1960's. The runways made excellent surfaces for motor car racing, attracting many enthusiasts to these popular sporting events. The driving surfaces were perfect for speed, and with great viewing for spectators, made exciting entertainment for families moving forward from the dark years of austerity that lingered on, long after the war ended.

A short stretch of runway was used after that time as a parachute drop zone but most of the land now has been taken over by agricultural industrialists who have made good use of the surrounding site.

Battle Headquarters at RAF Kinnell - Photograph courtesy of M Craib

Today, the Battle Headquarters for the air station remains in relatively good condition. During the wartime period this crucial structure would be situated at a distance from the runways, and if the airfield was under attack, the senior personnel on duty would conduct operations from this underground base. Currently, the structure can be located in the garden of a private residential dwelling, situated on the periphery of the site.

Jim Wallace, a resident of nearby Chapelton, recollects how busy the airfield at Kinnell was, with planes flying over day and night. He remembers vividly seeing a plane crashing in a field opposite Boysack Mill. A few days later, he and some of his school friends went across the field to look at the wreckage, as young lads would do, fully expecting to see a German fighter plane, but was saddened to see that it was one of our own aircraft, likely a trainee pilot who had lost his direction.

Henry 'Hank' Adlam also writes in his memoir *On and Off the Flight Deck* a brief but clear recollection of being a pilot at Kinnell which stood him in good stead for having a successful career, well into the post-war period, as a pilot with the Royal Navy. One can visualise these young chaps taking off and landing time and again, with little changes to the airfield itself today, amid the surrounding landscape which can change so rapidly with weather conditions.

There remains evidence of derelict wartime structures and although the runways remain surprisingly, in a relatively decent condition, the roadway leading from Kinnell to the Montreathmont junction, does now cut straight through the site. What is remarkable from that position is, it offers an unobstructed view of the flat landscape. One can easily visualise day and night time practice flying by young inexperienced pilots, during that bleak period of significant unrest under a constant threat of attack from enemy forces.

Close to RAF Kinnell lies rural Friockheim. Originally named Friock, (Gaelic - fraoch) meaning heather), the village was designed and built in 1814 by the Laird of the Lands of Friock, Mr Thomas Gardyne of Middleton. It became home to many flax textile workers who came to work in the various mills at Friock and nearby Colliston,; Leysmill; Hatton; Hattonden; Gightyburn and Boysack, where sailcloth and rope-making were the popular end products. The village of Friock, was then known as Friock Feus, as it was leased to Mr John Andson of Arbroath who was involved with the flax milling industry. 'Heim' – German for home, was added to Friock by Mr Andson's son, following his travels through Germany, where he had noticed many towns and villages had 'heim' as a suffix. With the Laird's permission, Friock was then named Friockheim from 1824 and remains so.

A Prisoner of War camp was situated on the edge of the village which housed initially Italian and German POWs. The camp was identified as *Kinnell Camp No 27/27A*, and lay a short distance from the airfield. There were two large huts and two smaller for accommodation and administration needs, which are documented on the UK sites *List of POW Camps*.

Today, there is no physical evidence of the site remaining, but some elderly residents of the village can remember the presence of POWs working in the fields. Agricultural workers were in short supply during the war years and POWs were allowed to work outwith the camp, as long as it was not directly involved with the war effort (*Geneva Convention regulations*). Many were selected to work with local farmers and were paid similar wages to British workers, although their freedom was obviously restricted. Those with inherent Nazi philosophies were not considered for this liberty, yet there are some artefacts adorned with swastikas, displayed in local Angus museums, which would indicate followers of the Nazi regime were also present in the Angus countryside. In 1943, Italian POWs began to be repatriated, with Germans continuing on site until 1946, although many enjoyed the lifestyle and continued to live in the community making Angus their new home.

Jim Wallace remembers the POW's he met, being pleasant lads who worked hard on the land. They were treated very well, both at the camp and by the local people. Wartime life in rural areas was far removed from the big cities. Jim remembers there always being plenty of fresh food, eggs, milk, cheese, chickens, vegetables, bread and everyone kept a pig. No one went hungry, despite the national rationing, but their country living lifestyle had likely always been that way – war or not.

CHAPTER 8 - RAF EDZELL

Maintenance Command

56°48'33.69 N 2°36'19.35 W

The military air station at Edzell was commissioned during WWI, being operational with a single landing strip in early 1918. By July, the facility was used as a single seat fighter training unit, until the school disbanded in 1919.

During the 1930's *expansion period*, the site was selected for further development. By combining a number of surrounding agricultural fields, this allowed for the construction of additional permanent runways and dispersal areas complete with enough hangars to accommodate a large number of aircraft. At the time of the hostilities starting, some buildings continued to remain in an incomplete state with essential services such as electricity and sewerage still to be installed. Early 1940, the first Hurricane aircraft arrived and was housed in an unfinished 'K' Type hangar, with others swift to follow. Time was of the essence to get this air station into operational function.

Edzell communications - photograph courtesy of M Craib

No 8 Flying Training School, based at nearby Montrose, was one of the busiest flying training centres in the country and by June 1940, Edzell became one of its first satellite stations. The SFTS strength then was utilised between RAF Montrose, Edzell and neighbouring air station, RAF Stracathro. Following the Battle of Britain, there was a requirement by the Air Ministry to replace the substantial losses experienced, in human and physical terms. The skies over Angus being less busy than those over other parts of the country, with coastal weather conditions and challenging landscape, made for ideal training opportunities for novice pilots.

By August 1940, Edzell became the base for the RAF's No 44 Maintenance Unit, whose primary function was to repair damaged aircraft of various types, make them fit for purpose, then distribute them to where they were needed within the shortest of time spans.

The MU carried out repairs and modifications to aircraft and their engines, often working collaboratively with civilian contractors, Cunliffe-Own Aircraft Ltd and Scottish Aviation Ltd. The aircraft establishment had increased substantially to include Oxfords, Wellingtons and Proctors flying in by October of 1940.

Edzell aircraft taxiway from the runway to the hangars on the right - photograph A Wood
Wikimedia Commons/Public Domain

Manpower was in significant short supply so the air station defences were augmented with a detachment of the Black Watch occupying strong points around the perimeter and manning a searchlight at night constantly remaining vigilant for any glider landings. High on the hillside north of the airfield, two Howitzers were stationed which was fairly typical of the type of artillery used to defend the Scottish airfields at that time.

By April 1942, the SFTS became No2 Flying Instructors School with Edzell as one of the many various satellite air stations and was in use until the war ceased in 1945. The layout suited the training task especially for Oxfords and Masters aircraft. The site also was a storage area for aircraft, releasing them when required for bases over the country.

Maintenance building at Edzell - photograph courtesy of M Craib

Many different types of aircraft passed through the air station at Edzell with a total of 348 being recorded in 1942. Finally, in that year, the concrete and tarmac surfaced runways were completed allowing further extension of the services provided on site.

By the end of 1915, the total stock of aircraft at Edzell was eight hundred and nineteen prior being transfered to other sites. MU No 44 continued in the post war period with Dakotas passing through the site. In October1951, No 612 Squadron flew Vampires from the site before finally returning to Dyce in Aberdeenshire in 1952. The MU had a five-year workplan, continuing to be operational until 1957 and also the No 662 Gliding School which had arrived from nearby Fordoun air station, a satellite for Montrose remained for a further three years before moving to Arbroath.

Local man Peter Cowie who currently is a volunteer at the Arbroath Elliot ROC post can recollect seeing aircraft fly in and out of the Edzell base as a young boy as can Jim Wallace, from Chapelton, who can also remember watching an aircraft being on fire at the site. Casualties were often flown into Edzell or nearby RAF Stracathro then transferred to the local hospital for treatment. An exciting time for young boys who could watch the activities from the boundary.

The air station continued to be under military control, eventually handing-over to the United States Navy, who then assumed administration of the site for long-range electronic surveillance by the American National Security Agency. The air station then adopted large circular white *golf ball* communication aerials which were identifiable from some distance and an elevated level of security was assumed by the USN authorities. This was the period of the Cold War and secrecy was imperative. The base eventually ceased to function and closed down in 1996.

Edzell - Communication Aerials - Photograph Writer's Own

CHAPTER 9 - RAF STRACATHRO

Flying Training Command – Flying Instructors School – Satellite Site

56°46'31.61 N 2°37'12.96 W

This wartime airfield is situated close to Edzell and lies approximately 4 miles north of Brechin, inland from Montrose. Approval was obtained in March 1939 for the acquisition of land at Stracathro to be developed as a Relief Landing Ground for nearby RAF Montrose Air Station. On aerial maps, photographs taken by German reconnaissance in September 1940, class it as *Brechin Airfield* due to its proximity to the town. The airfield started off simply as an oval, flat piece of land with a grass landing strip runway with little else, other than a few blister hangars. By June 1940, the site was used extensively by No8 Service Flying Training School from Montrose which had in excess of 100 Masters aircraft at its peak.

With the Grampian Mountains lying to the west, this airfield sits in a valley surrounded by fertile agricultural land and is almost square in its layout. During the wartime period, a concrete track was built around three of its sides and a total of eight Blister hangars were erected. Controlled by RAF Montrose, the first recorded flight was on16th May 1941. Around two hundred service personnel were involved with this busy airfield, being transported from their base at Montrose, as there were no accommodation blocks built on site. Night time flying as well as day flights were practised and it was heavily defended with machine gun posts against enemy attack.

Gun emplacement at RAF Stracathro -Photograph courtesy of Michael Craib

Stanton Air Shelter at Stracathro - photograph courtesy of M Craib

In 1942, the airfield was used by No 2 Flying Instructors School until 1944, affiliated to No 1541 Blind Approach Training Flight, with six Oxford aircraft in May 1943. In December of that year, an Oxford and a Hurricane collided over the airfield killing the two occupants in the Oxford. This was a site not bereft of tragedy given its small size, however this unit remained active at Stracathro until July 1945 when it was finally disbanded.

Machine Gunnery Position Stracathro - photograph courtesy of M Craib

Post war, Stracathro airfield was used as a satellite for No 44 Maintenance Unit based at Edzell for aircraft storage also No 260 MU based at Errol, midway between Dundee and Perth, for the storage of equipment and the site finally closed in 1948.

RAF Stracathro Power House - photograph courtesy of M Craib

Stracathro airfield was situated conveniently close to Stracathro House, a Grade A listed Palladium Mansion House built in 1847 by Archibald Simpson, and in whose grounds was based one of the country's seven Emergency Hospital Service facilities, to receive and treat military casualties from the start of the war in 1939.

Single storey wards were constructed to house up to 1000 patients, whilst the mansion house was made available to provide accommodation for the hospital staff. The first casualties came from the air raid on Montrose in 1940, followed by civilian casualties from London, Birmingham and Coventry. Injured service personnel from all theatres of war were received for treatment with the majority arriving by rail via Brechin Station. The more serious casualties were flown in directly to the airfield. Local man Jim Wallace clearly recollects as a child watching planes landing at Stracathro with casualties being transferred for treatment.

In the post war period, the hospital became part of the National Health Service in 1948, where it was classed as a *rural general* and today following much refurbishment, is a Scottish Regional Treatment Centre which caters for patients from NHS Tayside and Grampian.

Stracathro Mansion House - used as staff residences for the Hospital from 1938 - 2002 now is privately owned Photograph by Cisco Wikimedia Commons/ Public Domain

The Angus Radio Controlled Model Flying Club finally made some use of the airfield since the end of the wartime hostilities, but largely the airfield resumed its agriculture status.

Several military structures still survive on the periphery of the site of the airfield, including a good example of a Stanton Air Raid Shelter which is still in a reasonable condition.

CHAPTER 10 RAF TEALING

Flying Training Command – Advanced Flying Unit – Satellite Station

56°31'17.49 N 2°59'09.01 W

'I cannot forecast to you the action of Russia. It is a riddle wrapped in a mystery inside an enigma.' - *Winston Churchill in a Broadcast 1st October 1939.*

A new organisation for the initial training of pilots and observers had been introduced by the end of 1939 and this had four stages:

1. ITW.   Initial Training Wing – this consisted of basic physical and barrack drill plus the introduction to signals; navigation; map reading and the history and theory of flight.
2. EFTS.   Elementary Flying Training School – this consisted of advanced theory and basic flying, using simple training aircraft.
3. SFTS.   Service Flying Training School – this had advanced trainer aircraft – this was when the trainees gained their *wings*
4. OTU.   Operational Training Unit – this was where pilots met up with navigators; wireless operators and air gunners from their respective specialised schools.

The training at an OTU was like a post graduate course where all staff were qualified.   Crews were formed and trained together to fly in an operational squadron.

The village of Tealing is situated at the foot of the Sidlaw Hills about

6 miles north of Dundee, close to Forfar. In 1941, approval was given for the acquisition of land to construct an air station as the site was deemed suitable *'being an open expanse of agricultural land lying on level ground.'* Its location was perfect lying relatively close to the other Angus airfields and to the city of Dundee with its good transport links and military bases on the river Tay.

On the local website, a resident of Tealing, Mrs Ethel Hunter (nee Beattie) remembered in July 1940, officials approaching her parents at their farm and being told *'in the interests of national security they would erect poles at regular intervals in their fields to prevent enemy gliders landing'*. A year later, the same officials from the Air Ministry, requisitioned the farm and remaining fields to build an air station as a base for fighter aircraft. The airfield took its name after Kirkton of Tealing, which was situated just to the north of the area of farmland selected for the site.

RAF Tealing, opened on the 27th March 1942 as an Operational Training Unit which was equipped with Hurricanes; Masters and Lysander aircraft. The construction was fairly standard with only two concrete runways, eight Blister hangars were situated at various dispersal areas plus three T2 Bellman hangars in the main technical support area. Communal and recreational buildings were placed approximately two miles east of the military zone and reportedly many fine evenings of entertainment were spent on site with dances, concert parties with guests arriving from Dundee.

The proximity of the *Sidlaws (range of hills north of Dundee)* presented significant challenges for young trainee pilots, combined with the fog rolling in from the River Tay causing poor visibility on many occasions, making operational missions difficult. Night flying for novice pilots was considered to be impossible under these conditions.

The main priority for the Air Ministry was the construction of OTU airfields due to the rapid development of aircraft and the need for qualified pilots. This increase in training requirements brought with it the need for synthetic training aids to simulate flying; navigation; bombing and air gunnery. Tealing had a trainer which consisted of' *'a fuselage mounted on top of two pillars and the aircraft instrument panel was fitted with fully functional devices to simulate flight. The crew sat in their usual positions which enabled them, to train for circumstances such as engine fire; crash landing; ditching and parachuting under instruction. The instructor also had a similar panel so a number of complicated situations could be practiced safely'*. This trainer provided realistic simulation of operational flight – right from orders in the crew room through to completion of the combat report at the conclusion. The Edmonds Deflection Trainer was used for the training of fighter pilots *in aircraft recognition, range judging and deflection shooting using a standard Link Trainer which was fitted with a spotlight and reflector sight. This was operated by the pilot firing a button on the control column.*

Joe Ingram, fondly remembers RAF Tealing in his memoir *Whither Wings* and recollects receiving specialist instruction on the synthetic flying instrument trainer. Joe's first encounter with the RAF was '*attending a meeting at the Marryat Hall in Dundee where speakers were appealing for recruitment for service in the RAF regaling the young audience on tales of glamour and tours of distant lands with training and opportunities beyond their dreams.*' Volunteers for aircrew were in great demand and the success of the Battle of Britain aroused the ambition of many of the local lads '*with the desire to be a spitfire pilot.*' Joe was one of them and he went on to have a distinguished career in the service.

On the 20th May 1942, an unusual four engine bomber of Russian design and manufacture appeared out of the clouds. Eyewitnesses are reported to recollect '*hearing the aircraft approaching and watching it skirt low over the city of Dundee, before coming down to land at the air station'*. It is also reported that '*the locals had never seen anything like it… the sheer size and presence of the bomber…*' The very important passenger the crew were escorting was Vycheslav Molotov, the Russian Foreign Minister and Deputy of the State Committee of Defence, who was accompanied by sixteen Soviet officials, on a military assignment to meet with Winston Churchill in London. His mission was to conduct urgent negotiations with Britain and the United States to form wartime alliances. He was a tough negotiator, also a determined defender of Soviet interests.

Derelict Control Tower at RAF Tealing - Photograph – Courtesy of M Craib

Russian Bomber Petlyakov Pe-8 (TB7) at RAF Tealing - Wikimedia Commons/Public Domain

Molotov had replaced Litvinov, the more moderate Soviet Foreign Minister on the 4th May 1938 and was known for his brutal, hard line tactics. Winston Churchill in his wartime memoirs acknowledged him as *'a man of outstanding ability and cold-blooded ruthlessness.'*

The invasion of Russia by German forces from June 1941, found Britain with an ally opportunity on the eastern front which removed the threat of imminent invasion of our coasts. However, in the event of Russia being defeated, Britain would be left in a far more vulnerable situation. Churchill recognised the risk and offered assistance to the Russians even though British resources, especially armaments, were stretched to their limits. To formalise the conditions, it was necessary for Russia to sign the pact, hence the secret mission to transport Molotov to Britain to sign the Treaty of Alliance, linking the two world powers.

RAF Tealing was selected to be the most suitable landing site for security purposes, as it would attract as little attention as possible. The aircraft that flew in to the small air station was a giant *Petlyakov Pe-8 (TB7) Long-range Strategic Heavy Russian bomber*, which flew directly from Russia over the Baltic, north of Denmark and across the North Sea. This was a dangerous and courageous mission for both the aviators and Molotov as a key figure in the Soviet Government to make, given the risks of flying directly over enemy territory.

News of Molotov's visit was *blacked out* under the severe war restrictions, certainly for at least several weeks. Information, however, filtered out through sources who indicated he had been seen in the city, then had travelled from Dundee Station to London by train. This was supported by witness statements of local residents *'of seeing Russian officials being lodged at the Royal Hotel in Dundee for several days and also observing their presence, with local police, along the south-bound platform at the railway station.'* Such news leaked out to the *press* and still can be found documented in many articles and books available through archives, however as we now have todays access to released wartime records, we find out that was actually not the case and what we today would class as *fake news!*

Recent documentation, released from military authorities indicate that this was part of a deception plan put in place for security purposes. Molotov and his officials had essentially been collected from RAF Tealing in *Minerva Limo*usines hired from a Dundee firm, W.P. Robertson and driven to Errol Airfield, some 11 miles west of Dundee. This was where Molotov made a split-second decision which ultimately saved his life.

Molotov with Churchill at 10 Downing Street Gardens May 1942 - Photograph: Dept of Foreign Affairs and Trade – Wikimedia Commons/Public Domain

He was offered the choice of two aircraft to fly onwards to London for his meeting with British officials. The one he did not select, crashed over the Vale of York, killing his support staff as well as senior RAF officers who were accompanying. Molotov did, however, arrive safely for the signing of the Anglo-Russian Treaty which took place on the 26th May 1942. After spending valuable time in discussion with Winston Churchill, he then went on to fly to Washington to meet with US President Roosevelt.

'I have never seen a human being who more perfectly represented the modern conception of a robot' *The Second World War, Vol 1: Winston Churchill*

A little bit of excitement for the small air station at Tealing. The auspicious event being commemorated some decades after the end of World War II, by the erection of a stone memorial situated outside the village hall.

After this thrilling interlude, the daily business of training pilots for wartime duties continued as usual. The initial forty trainees based on site rapidly increased to one hundred and fifty by the following year. Many of the instructors of the novice pilots also held an operational role known as 556 Squadron, which was part of the Peterhead sector, providing escorts for convoys and reconnaissance duties over the North Sea.

More than eighty Hawker Hurricane fighters operated from this airfield at its peak being classed as a *very busy flying training unit.'* RAF Tealing then had RAF Kinnell as its satellite site from March to October 1943. During that time, RAF Tealing became No 1 Tactical Exercise Unit (TEU) controlled under the Combat Training Wing which specialised in *air-firing and evasive action,* By the end of the year there were over one hundred aircraft based on the site.

In the early months of 1944, RAF Tealing exchanged forty Hurricanes for thirty-eight Spitfires which had been based at Grangemouth, near Stirling. The air station was then placed on high alert and made fully operational ready, anticipating an attack by enemy forces invading from occupied Norway. Preparations also gave a clear signal of a build-up of fighter strength as part of an Allied Forces plan. The TEU disbanded on the 3st July, but during their final period, hosted Dakotas, which arrived over the course of a five-day period which were used to shuttle local troops to the south of Britain to reinforce the allied advance in Normandy. The busiest day recorded was the 31st, when ninety Dakotas made the trip from RAF Tealing to the airborne operations airfields located in the Cotswolds.

August 1944 saw RAF Tealing under the control of Flying Training

Command with No 9 Advanced Flying Unit based at Errol as its Relief Landing Ground. The trainers of this unit started from September and continued operations until 21 June 1945 thereafter the air station was placed as a Maintenance Unit under the control of RAF Montrose for a short period of time. With hostilities coming to an end, it was decided there would be no post-war future for the site and it eventually closed.

Today, some military buildings remain in situ including the control tower which is sadly in a derelict state and the runways have now returned to an agricultural function.

CHAPTER 11 – RAF FORDOUN (Aberdeenshire)

Flying Training Command – Satellite to RAF Montrose

56°52'38.63 N 2°24'59.89 W

'In wartime....truth is so precious that she should always be attended by a bodyguard of Lies.'

Winston Churchill - Tehran Conference 1943

Geographically, this wartime air station was not situated in the county of Angus rather it can be found a handful of miles crossing the county boundary into Aberdeenshire, formerly known as Kincardineshire. Because of its significant contribution as a satellite site, also its valuable contribution to aerial warfare, it would be appropriate to include in this edition.

1941 saw the acquisition of land at Fordoun for the construction of an airfield primarily as a satellite for Montrose and Peterhead, on the north of the village. It was an ideal location, being a rural agricultural setting with flat open fields and little habitation. The site had a two concrete runway system with the option to expand should it be necessary, with accommodation for four Blister hangars, communal and technical buildings.

RAF Fordoun Operations Building - photograph courtesy of M Craib

RAF Fordoun opened as a satellite for No2 Flying Instructors School at RAF Montrose, with Oxfords and Masters from November 1942, thereafter came Hawker Hurricanes, Miles Martinets and Westland Lysanders which were used for gunnery practice and radar calibration testing.

Nissen Huts at Fordoun - photograph courtesy of M Craib

An exceptional formation of 'non-operational type' aircraft were also housed on this site from 1943. These were dummy *Douglas Bostons*.

Dummy Boston Aircraft example - photograph from Pinterest

This was part of the clever military deception plan - *Operation Tyndall*, with RAF Fordoun being one of the sites selected in Scotland to be used for this purpose. Military deception tactics were exceptionally effective when used against enemy forces during WWII and they were ramped up specifically in preparation for the allied invasion. In Britain, the D-Day deception plan was codenamed *Operation Fortitude,* being part of the larger, overall UK deception strategy, known as- *Operation Bodyguard.*

Operation Bodyguard was organised in two parts – ***North*** – designed to fool the Germans into believing the allied forces would launch an attack on Norway. The use of RAF Fordoun as a site was perfect for this purpose given its situation within easy flying distance from the Norwegian coast. This entailed placing volumes of the dummy aircraft at the airfield to assume a build-up of resources in preparation of a full-on allied assault, thus masking the true operational objective hence giving the added element of surprise. ***South*** – indicating a planned offensive across the English Channel to Calais, thus diverting attention from the actual invasion site of Normandy.

In 1944, No5 Gliding School was formed at this location in October and was operational on site until 1946, before moving to Dyce, which is located north of Aberdeen city. In the post war period, the airfield was used briefly from August 1945 until August of the following year as a satellite for No 98 Maintenance Unit for the storage of explosives and in

87

later years for the storage of ammunition.

Blister Hangar at Fordoun used for agricultural purposes - photograph taken in 2005 courtesy of M Craib

Fordoun Airfield Fire Station - photograph courtesy of M Craib

Flying came to an end as a result of the runway surfaces starting to crack, although repairs were indeed carried out to ensure stability. Eventually the airfield ceased to function on the 30th September 1950.

The airfield had not seen the end of its flying days as in May 1965 it reopened for private flying with it being the base for the Fordoun Flying Club in 1967. By the early 1970's its use changed again, this time being

88

used as a stock car racing circuit but following a fatal accident once again was closed down.

The facility nowadays is used for the storage of oil industry equipment; however, the runways and taxi track are still visible. Unfortunately, as a consequence of a fire, the Blister Hangars have now collapsed but the remains of Nissen Huts, Stanton airfield shelters and operational buildings are still visible, but in a derelict state.

CHAPTER 11 – Buddon

Army Training Camp - Satellite

56°29'03.00 N 2°46'42.11 W'

There has been an Army base situated at Buddon since the 19th century with the land at Barry being sold to the War Office by Lord Panmure in 1897 for use as a military training centre. Buddon was also the satellite site for RNAS Stannergate at Dundee, a seaplane base, which operated from WWI and saw active service through WWII. Located on the northeast coastal edge of Angus, close to the town of Carnoustie, the base lies adjacent to the famous golf links and has seen active service throughout both world wars.

Prior to WWI, the base was used primarily for the training of troops in preparation for the anticipated hostilities and there are some fascinating artefacts in existence. A box system of WWI trenches was found by archaeologists, hidden under overgrown shrubland on the site. Following excavation, these training trenches, which run from Barry Ridge to Barry Links, date from WWI times and show a variety of *military trench construction techniques including the use of breastwork style parapets. The overall complex is designed to enable multiple activities to run concurrently within the complex with the ability for the movement of troops around communication support trenches.*

Among the artefacts found were sandbags, fire steps and WWI cartridge shells one of which dates from a Martini Henry rifle from the Anglo-Zulu war in 1879, however, the majority having been shot from various rifles, including the *Enfield* type.

Archaeologist standing in the training trench system - note sandbags in layers lining the trench walls - photograph taken by Writer with permission for use from MOD and Wessex Archaeology team 2019

These training trenches were used by troops before they were deployed to France and Belgium. The system which was excavated in 2019 is a complex layout of trenches and communication channels where the evidence of sandbag-built walls gives the archaeological team the theory that these are *breastworks*, a type of trench built for use in Belgium where the ground was sodden. Phil Abramson, a senior archaeologist with the Defence Infrastructure Organisation (DIO) a part of the Ministry of Defence (MOD) who own the site, indicates 'excavations reveal the trench system soldiers trained in before going to fight on the front lines of the First World War...and the team hope to return next year as they feel the site still has a lot of secrets to give up.' Unfortunately there are no photographs available of the soldiers at practice in these trenches, but Chairman of the Carnoustie British Legion, Dave Paton, agrees 'it is fascinating to have such an insight into how troops lived and fought..... made all the more poignant by the discovery of articles of military equipment and personal effects that the team had uncovered during their excavations.'

WAR DOG TRAINING AT BUDDON

During the WWI years, the base at Buddon also had a further significant training function – to train dogs. Throughout history, dogs have been used in conflict situations as far back as ancient Greeks and Romans, whose Generals recognised their value in the battlefield. Dogs hold a certain intelligence and obedience to follow instructions, coupled with their courage and determination to complete their set task, made them a crucial cog in the war machine. The training of such dogs was the lifelong vocation of Lt Colonel Edwin Richardson, who lived in nearby Panbride House. His input and tenacity led to the involvement of canines in the front lines of trench warfare by training them to run messages, seek and find wounded soldiers, carry first-aid pouches and make for excellent patrol and guard duties. Richardson trained these dogs on the beaches at East Haven and Carnoustie with the assistance of many local residents acting as wounded in the sand dunes.

The officers at Barry Buddon Army Training Camp allowed him access with his dogs to train with the men as ambulance dogs. The Airedale Terrier was the dog group selected predominantly, but others were also just as competent for the task. It is documented that the terriers carried small flasks of whisky in their sacks. Needless to say, this form of exercise was much appreciated by the troops. The dogs worked under combat conditions, being trained to run wearing gas masks and ignoring the firing guns of any calibre and grenade explosion. The commanding officers were sufficiently impressed with the dogs' performance; indeed, they notified the War Office to advise them making recommendation for the use of these war dogs, as they worked wonderfully and were indispensable in conditions of warfare. Those dogs could run fast through the communication trenches delivering messages and supplies and were seen to be a valuable resource during the hostilities.

Large quantities of dogs were required to be trained, as they were quick to learn, fierce and swift. The War Office requested Richardson to set up the British War Dog Training School at Shoeburyness, Essex, with dogs supplied by Battersea Dogs Home plus other rescue centres. No-one could doubt the dangerous conditions these brave animals worked in with many being killed in action, only known by the numbers on their collars. It wasn't until 2006 that the wearing of a purple poppy then became a symbol of remembrance for animals who served during wartime.

In memory of their vast contribution, the Airedale Terrier Club of Scotland commissioned a granite monument, designed and carved by Scottish sculptor, Bruce Walker, which was unveiled at East Haven beach in 2019. A fitting tribute which acknowledges the sacrifices made by dogs during this conflict, situated in the area where the war dog training was established.

Memorial to the War Dogs - photograph Writers own – taken 2019

The military site at Buddon was also used as a WWI and WWII satellite site for the seaplane base at Dundee where patrols along the North Sea coastline took place. Buddon being situated north of the river Tay estuary provided landing site availability on the coast. On the inland side of the military buildings, there is a wide-open expanse which looks out towards the golf courses and town of Carnoustie. This would be the likely airfield runway site given its location and situation.

A rare find was a gun turret from WWII situated on the southern aspect of the rectangular layout. At first it looked remarkably like an *Alan Williams turret* which excited the Archaeology team but sadly, although very similar, the cupola did not rotate and was one of a type used on coastal defences over Scotland. One similar also is still sited at Tentsmuir, overlooking the site of former RAF Leuchars in Fife. The turret at Buddon is in a derelict, fragile condition, nevertheless, it indicates the structure was once an armoured observation point, ready to attack enemy forces. Its proximity also indicates the trenches may have been viable for use as local defence during WWII. A pillbox situated within a group of trees and a concrete shuttered bunker with two observation slits are also surviving military structures on this site.

Cuppola at Buddon -photograph Writers Own taken 2019

More recently, on the 1st and 2nd May 1966, 600 troops were landed at the army training camp from the assault ship HMS Fearless, supported

94

by two Wessex helicopters operating from the ship's flight deck. Their mission was to construct an airstrip complete with emergency bulk fuel installations within a two- week period. From the 13th May, several take-offs and landings then took place from the packed sand surface. This was the first time a temporary airfield project of this extent had been attempted in Britain. The airfield continued to be used until 1976 in liaison with the army training camp.

Currently, Barry Buddon' is a Ministry of Defence modern military facility, which includes rifle ranges, excellent accommodation and training amenities for todays forces. Gary Archer, Safety Training Officer at the base on discovering the trenches and artefacts, affirms it would be great to *'redevelop the area and restore it to its former glory...... it would be an asset to the camp for education purposes and historical context.'* A heartening worthwhile assignment linking the heritage of the past to the future of the base.

Front opening of Turret - photograph Writers Own taken 2019

CHAPTER 13

COASTAL DEFENCE - EVOLUTION OF RADAR

Communications and early detection of enemy activity were vital for the military, with the small county of Angus, playing a significant role in this field from the 1930's *Expansion Period* throughout WWII, and continuing into the Cold War time zone. Wireless transmission was in its infancy since the early twentieth-century, with *Guglielmo Marconi* taking credit for the first transatlantic wireless transmission on December 12 1901. A magnificent achievement of its time which was destined to change the world forever.

During WWI years, communications were basic still with the use of hand delivery, carrier pigeon or dogs as message carriers. Wireless development had progressed but its use was variable under the prevailing conditions of the period, however, as the years advanced, the technology of the time did likewise.

British messenger dogs with their handler in France during WWI - National Library of Scotland - Wikimedia Commons - Flickr - Public Domain

It was Angus scientist, *Robert Watson-Watt*, from Brechin, who advanced the use of the technology that allows the transmission of sound or other signals by modulation of electro-magnetic waves (radio) via wireless, the medium of radio communication - the pioneer of *RADAR* (Radio Detection and Ranging).

Knowledge of radar was out there in the scientific community but Watson-Watt's genius lay that he alone identified the possibilities it provided, and knew how it could work to our country's advantage. He was confident that equipment could be designed and developed, using the principle of radio detection, to provide the solution to the fundamental problem of the nation's defence. The work of Arnold Wilkins confirmed this.

In 1934, RAF fighter pilots could not intercept incoming enemy aircraft, and in a small island nation where no place is more than 15 minutes flying time from the coast, a system was required which could detect attack providing early warning and allowing time for pilots to become airborne.

A minimum of 20 minutes notice would be required and Watson-Watt, with the support of the Air Ministry, prepared a series of experiments to allow this to happen.

Memorial to Sir Robert Watson-Watt located at Brechin - Photograph Writer's Own taken 2019

The development of radar as a defence mechanism was researched at Bawdsey Research Station in Suffolk, with steel masts at Orford Ness being erected to detect incoming marauding aircraft from distances from the coastline. With tensions increasing over the swift rise in Hitler's dominating powers over Europe and with anxiety over the threat of impending war for the second time in recent history, there was now a sense of urgency for the need to protect this island nation once again.

By 1937, Watson-Watt had established a system of *Chain Home Radar Stations* initially along the vulnerable south-east coast of England. A survey was completed in 1938 to assess the suitability of the terrain for air defence radar, which resulted in the rapid increase of these new stations by the start of war in 1939, which would encompass the coastal regions of Britain, thus forming a curtain of radar detection.

The east coastal stations were of similar design to the *experimental site* at *Bawdsey* except these were now developed to have equipment housed in protective buildings with transmitter aerials suspended from 350ft steel towers and receiver aerials mounted on 240ft timber frames.

The tall radio masts at Orford Ness Suffolk -Photograph by Keith Evans- Wikimedia Commons/Public Domain

The majority of the *Chain Home Stations* were also provided with reserve equipment which was either based remotely or housed underground. The underground reserve consisted of a transmitter and receiver block each with three entrance hatches, (two for equipment and one for personnel) which were set on steel rollers with emergency exit hatches, ventilation shafts and a 120ft wooden tower carrying the aerials. Most stations were powered from the *National Grid*, but these, like those without mains supply access, had generators to cover any interruption in supply. These were located in a separate protected building known as the *stand-by set house.*

Research by Watson-Watt and his team of scientists continued during the early war years to include the development of a radar system small enough and accurate for a fighter pilot to detect night time enemy bombers approaching the coast. During early experiments, RAF pilots noticed they could fly undetected when they flew at low altitude, and if they could, then so could the enemy.

A series of *Chain Home Low* stations were then built in various vulnerable situations between the *Chain Home* network of high antennae radar. These were manually operated systems that required operators to *seek* for targets by having moving the antenna back and forward and monitoring for returns on screen.

Interior of the transmitter room in a typical CHL Station 1939-1945 - RAF Official Photographer- CH15184 IWM - Wikimedia Commons/Public Domain

There can be no doubt that without the scientific knowledge, skill and determination of this Angus born pioneering engineer who was educated at the University College of Dundee, linked to the University of St Andrews, the Battle of Britain in 1940 could have had a very different outcome. After the bombing of Pearl Harbour in 1941, Watson-Watt was dispatched to the United States to assist them with radar detection. He was celebrated by receiving a knighthood from *King George VI* in 1944 and freedom of the *Cathedral City* of Brechin. His outstanding achievements are commemorated by the erection of a memorial which depicts him holding a Spitfire in one hand and a radio antenna in the other.

WAAF Radar Operator Denise Miley plotting aircraft on a cathode ray tube in the Receiver Room at Bawdsey Chain Home Station in May 1945- Photograph from Wikimedia Commons/ Public Domain

World War II witnessed the greatest mobilisation of women in history for service in the Armed Forces. The Women's Auxiliary Air Force was created in July 1939 to take on non-combatant war duties, such as clerical, catering, store-keeping, message-relaying, etc vital to the efficiency of the service. By 1940, women were trained in the role of aircraft plotting and utilising their communications skills, this made them invaluable however, their contribution, sadly has often been underestimated. By 1943, the WAAF made up 16% of RAF strength with many women working in remote air stations and rural bases.

CHAIN HOME RADAR STATIONS IN ANGUS

RAF DOUGLASWOOD –CHAIN HOME RADAR STATION NEAR MONIKIE

56°32'07.47 N 56° 33 2° 50 W

This base is one of a series of Chain Home Air Defence stations situated around the British coast which was equipped for use at the start of WWII in 1939. It gave an early warning of enemy aircraft approaching from a distance of eighty miles offshore e. Situated in a remote, sparsely populated area surrounded by dense woodland, this brick and concrete station was defended by five pillboxes on its perimeter. The four transmitter aerials were carried on 360ft steel lattice towers with similar but smaller 250ft receiver towers located at a distance further away.

On the 16th October 1939, Douglaswood was one of two radar stations that detected a formation of enemy bombers making its way towards the Forth estuary to attack the naval base and dockyard at Rosyth, located beyond the iconic Forth Bridge. This was the first air raid over the British Isles, and the first of many to follow.

The monitoring staff at Douglaswood also directed RAF Hurricanes and Spitfires onto enemy aircraft off the east coast intent on attacking shipping in April and May 1941. They were also instrumental for the alert and tracking of large formations of German bombers heading for Clydeside where horrendous damage to property and industry took place, leaving devastation and significant loss of lives.

A former RAF pilot from 1918 and one who served at Montrose Air Station in both world wars, recollects working at RAF Douglaswood. Lieutenant Archibald Laidlaw had been initially trained as a wireless operator in 1916 and became an expert in the new field of wireless technology. He set up his own business in Aberdeen in 1920, making and supplying wireless sets and found he had to travel to Germany to source some of the materials he required. There he met Erica Heller and they married in Berlin in 1933. As war was imminent, Laidlaw found his skills were required once again by the RAF. He initially worked on the new radar station at Douglaswood in 1938 making it fit for purpose and the following year he returned to RAF Montrose, where he served until the end of the war. His position as a technical expert who was involved with *secret equipment* and being married to a German woman at a time of war, presented them both with some extremely difficult situations to deal with given the level of anti-Nazi sentiment felt by locals.

Today, this now former radar station still retains several of its original war time buildings and features including mast supports and continues to be used by Dundee District Scout Council.

CHAIN HOME LOW RADAR STATIONS

RAF THE LAW - By Carnoustie and RAF ST CYRUS – Near Montrose

A Chain Home Low Radar Station can detect aircraft flying at low altitudes below the capability of the Chain Home radars. This high frequency radar used smaller antennae that could be swung back and forth to seek returns on the operator's screen, in contrast to the large mast fixed antennae used by the Chain Home stations.

At the start of the hostilities, the German bombers would fly almost all of their bombing raids at low altitude avoiding detection and was first noticed when German mine-laying aircraft were spotted flying low over the sea. Invariably these raids were never intercepted until often too late.

There can be no doubt that this form of low altitude detection by radar played a significant role in the Chain Home network and without it the Battle of Britain may have taken a different course.

CHAPTER 14
ANGUS SIGNAL INTERCEPTION STATIONS

MONTREATHMONT
Wireless Signal Interception Centre – 'PO Box 25'
56°40'08.60 N 2°40'32.20 W

These facilities were established to monitor radio traffic signals, then analyse their content locally to secure necessary intelligence and identify the source, prior to relaying them to the appropriate authority. Often the incoming information was encrypted which required decoding and relayed onto Britain's national Code and Cypher School at Bletchley Park.

Hidden from view within a forest about a mile from Kinnell air station, in the valley of Strathmore in central Angus, lies a mysterious building situated at the end of a single-track road. This secret location manned by purposely selected personnel, played a significant role in the WW II intelligence war. Addressed as *PO Box 25*, only a few individuals knew where this was, and what secret work was undertaken at this site. This was Montreathmont, whose covert function was crucial to the success of many clandestine missions and whose personnel were shrouded in secrecy.

As early as 1937, MI6 were investigating enemy infiltration into the country and the use of low power transmitters used by foreign agents who sent vital information or which acted as beacons for enemy aircraft attacks. Locating illicit transmissions was, at first, the role of the General Post Office (GPO), but with the threat of war and rapidly increasing developments, the military then assumed the responsibility for tracking and intercepting.

Montreathmont was the second largest listening post in Britain, controlled by the Radio Security Service (RSS) under the auspices of MI6, and its site suitability was owing to Brechin-born Captain Walter Robertson, who held experience in commanding the wireless listening station at Thurso, in Caithness. Having local knowledge, he was aware of the remote location and secluded surrounding area. On his advice, the RSS conducted a geographical survey which found the iron content in the soil provided metallic conditions which were beneficial for the purpose of increasing the efficiency of the aerial structure. The Angus site became fully operational in early 1943 to complement Hanslope Park Headquarters situated in Buckinghamshire, which was the military's major intelligence listening post. That site, due to its location, experienced many receiving difficulties, with incomplete and garbled information when listening in to Germany. This led to the requirement for a back-up station which could receive clear transmissions without interruptions in service and the north-east of Scotland was seen to be the ideal location for this significant role.

Manned by an ingenious team from the Royal Corps of Signals, they listened into transmissions from *Hitler's Bunker* daily and managed information from sites across Europe 24/7. This team of *'secret operatives'* held a substantial responsibility in the success of *'ULTRA'*, the name allotted to British Intelligence, as Montreathmont was one of the major sub-stations for *Bletchley Park*, (Station X), Britain's' code-breaking centre. Bletchley's success was a major break-through for the Allied forces however, the successful interception of enemy signals at Montreathmont, allowed the decoders to penetrate, analyse and decipher the German Enigma code.

The Special Communications Unit at Montreathmont was eighteen strong, receiving daily reports from Norwegian agents who were using low voltage transmitters, probably dropped off from the seaplanes which were based at RAF Woodhaven on the Fife side of the River Tay, near the city of Dundee. They also received messages from French Resistance fighters whose input increased as D-Day preparations were advanced. The operators often had very difficult messages intercepted, due to the transmission conditions of the time. They were a select set of individuals who worked within this '*secret site*', completely self-contained in their covert surroundings, and bound by the Official Secrets Act.

This 'top secret' listening post and decoding centre, listened to transmissions from '*German and Italian armed forces, the Gestapo, SS Officers, the Abwehr (German Secret Service) and from the bunker where Hitler's Generals received their orders.*' The '*interceptors*' also searched for and hunted out transmissions from '*German spies as well as Norwegian Resistance fighters.*' An example of the importance of covert communications was regarding the German battleship Tirpitz which was anchored near Tromso. Visual confirmation from agents on the ground, was required by the British War Cabinet to back up the photographic evidence already produced through ULTRA, before the order was sent to RAF Kinloss to release Lancaster bombers. Underground Norwegian agents provided that crucial information which was received and relayed from Montreathmont.

Montreathmont site was split into two distinct areas, with the two-storey, flat roofed, listening station situated at the top of the hill on Montreathmont Moor. Rising high above the tree line were the radio and transmitter aerial towers situated some distance from the fifty two code-breaking machines which ran continuously. These vastly noisy, mechanical appliances produced '*waste heat and noise – both acoustic and electrical*' which could have disrupted transmissions and interfered with listening if situated too close to the main building. These machines would likely have been similar to the 'British Bombe' type used and the dimensions would have been '*7ft wide; 6ft 6in tall and 2ft deep weighing a ton*'.

There was a '*direction finding aerial scanner*' installed on the flat roof and the signal operators worked on the ground floor accommodation. The upper level housed the map room, duty officer and other administrative quarters. There was also an enormous generator based at this installation keeping the power supply running continually to maintain this vital top-secret operation.

Antennae Mast at Montreathmont - Photograph courtesy of M Craib

Canadian Huts at Montreathmont - photograph courtesy of M Craib

The living accommodation was based far down the single-track road, approximately half a mile, close to the entrance of the site and at a distance where the noise of the machines could not be heard. There are reports of a total of four hundred Canadian and Polish personnel being based there with one hundred and fifty staff working at the listening station, however, there are also witness accounts which determine staff were actually billeted at Forfar, Brechin and as far out as Kirriemuir. During this 'secretive' wartime period, there was an element of disinformation about, what today we would class as *'fake news'* so indeed there may have been a combination of both.

Indeed, there remains evidence of accommodation blocks at the site. The *'Canadian Huts'* a type of Nissen hut with pronounced peaked, rounded roofs have maintained their unusual structure and are still in use by families today. There is evidence of brick-built wartime buildings such as a guard room and possible garage/storage facilities but their condition is sadly deteriorating.

108

Guard Room at Montreathmont and long driveway up to the station - Photograph courtesy of M Craib

It would be pertinent to mention that in addition to this professionally manned station, there were around fifteen hundred amateur voluntary radio '*interceptors*' who worked from their own homes and were spread out over the country, who played a decisive role in this subversive climate. These individuals were enlisted by the RSS to '*locate, listen and report*' the transmitters of enemy spies in Britain, and they were exceptional in their attention to detail. It is reported that '*every German agent was tracked, then caught and arrested by MI5*', which demonstrated a fierce level of commitment to duty.

The site was extended in the post WWII period then being staffed by civilian personnel and was renamed as the 'Diplomatic Listening Post'. Montreathmont continued to monitor communications during the 'Cold War' period. When the 20 plus radio masts were removed in 1966, the site then came under the administration of 'The Secretary of State for Scotland' for their own communication systems before eventual closure during the 1990's.

Montreathmont can also claim its' fame as Station X, featured in the movie 'Enigma' which was released in 2001.

Finally, the site at Montreathmont was put up for sale to be used for private dwelling. BBC News in April 2004, reported it as '*a former listening station which helped crack the Enigma Code used by Germans in the Second World War*'. Today, this most unusual site continues to be occupied, this time with families, far removed from the secrecy and intrigue associated with its past – although a fifty foot mast gives some notion of its former life.

'a nation can survive its fools and even the ambitious but it cannot survive treason from within. An enemy at the gate is less formidable, for he is known and carries his banner openly. But the traitor moves amongst those within the gate freely….'

Marcus Tullius Cicero 106-43 BC

The majority of citizens followed the maxims of *Business as Usual* and *Keep Calm and Carry On* providing the brave stoic attitude the British are renowned for but there was an underbelly whose allegiance lay with the country's enemies. These were people who worked alongside patriotic colleagues often invisible within the company of trusting others whilst they carried out their daily tasks. They were the most dangerous as they blended into surroundings remaining largely unnoticed. Their assignments were to seek out intelligence or commit acts of destructive sabotage to assist attacking forces who had the determination to invade our island shores.

There were also those with their own agenda, specifically those working in privileged positions within society. Individuals who were thought to have been beyond reproach – ones who had the ability to obtain vital sensitive information, yet be destructive when required, believing they would receive significant positions of power following what they anticipated would be a successful invasion.

Angus, being an area of military interest possessed plentiful stories about suspicious individuals considered as enemies of the state, but there are two high profile cases which shocked not only the county but the whole country. The first spotlights on a rather ordinary woman situated in an ordinary Scottish town.

Jessie Wallace was born in Glasgow in 1889, the illegitimate daughter of a housemaid and raised by her grandmother. Family life was brutal, dysfunctional and with little hope of her attaining any academic promise. She had relocated to Dundee by the age of twenty, unemployed with no prospects, when she met a young German called Fritz Jordan who was working as a waiter in the Royal Hotel.

Friendship turned to love and they were married in 1912 in Hanover. Jessie settled into German life and her daughter Margaretha was born at the start of WWI. When Fritz was called up for military service, Jessie moved to Hamburg where she started up a small business as a beautician and hairdresser. Life was difficult, she was British by birth but was classified as a German citizen and after Fritz died as a result of pneumonia following trench warfare, she returned to Dundee.

This was short lived as she could not settle and spent the next few years travelling to and from Hamburg. Her business acumen however escalated rapidly throughout the 1920's being successful managing several shops in the fashionable city suburbs. She became immensely popular within her own social circle catching the eye of Nazi officials which led her to make some dangerous connections. By mid-thirties, the Nazi party was in control of the country and life once again became complicated. Rising debts against large financial advances left her no option but to go into liquidation – her success had come to an abrupt end.

Back to Scotland in 1937 in a housekeeping situation in Perth for her stepbrother was too good an opportunity to miss, but when Nazi senior officials became aware of her departure, they also saw the prospect of her becoming valuable to their cause with her becoming an agent for the Abwehr.

Hamburg had a thriving secret service being ideally situated for observing maritime links between Britain and the United States, with agents in these two nations collecting substantial intelligence using a combination of mail and courier services. Jessie was recruited as a courier with the attraction of excitement, danger and 'easy money' enticing her to a life of deceit and espionage with her first assignment being to photograph, sketch plans and relay information on the Royal Armaments Depot at Crombie in Fife. One mission followed another with Jessie travelling across the country often with her stepbrother's children whom she took to the Angus beaches to collate information on the coastal defences and produce sketches of the military positions.

When Jessie spotted an advertisement for a hairdressing salon in Dundee being up for sale and reflecting on her previous successful ventures, she saw the freedom she now required to further her work for the Abwehr using the shop as an address for mail received from the United States which could be relayed onwards to Hamburg. Jessie was not the most attentive of spies and soon gave herself away by the most basic of errors by using an Abwehr address known to MI5. She also left evidence of her clandestine activities such as drawings of the Tay Bridge with the icon – Zeppelin and documents pertaining to the RAF base at Leuchars in Fife lying on the shop counter, noticed by staff who raised the alert.

Jessie had a suspicion that her mail was being tampered with so she opted to rent a small flat in Stirling Street close to the hairdressing premises but by this time she was now under surveillance. Careless behaviour by her leaving a map detailing coastal military installations lying around, led to the arrest of Jessie Jordan March 1938.

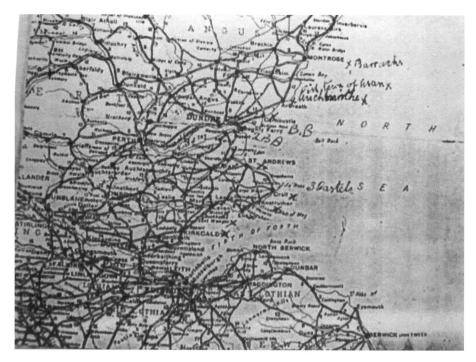

Map indicating military information - Jessie Jordan - photograph- Wikimedia Commons/Public Domain

Jessie denied all accusations but when presented with a plethora of evidence admitted her actions in providing shipping and military installation information acting as a go-between from United States spies to the German Secret Service. Coastal defence military facilities and batteries at Carnoustie, Broughty Ferry and those up the Angus coastline would have provided enemy forces a significant amount of detail for planning any future attack.

She was remanded in custody at Perth Prison while eighteen Abwehr agents, all of whom were named by her were arrested in America. The FBI stated 'the US involvement was the greatest spy-ring in peace time history.' At her trial in the High Court in Edinburgh, Jessie Jordan pleaded guilty to the conspiracy charges and was sentenced to four years imprisonment. When WWII hostilities commenced, Jessie was moved to Holloway Prison in London following the sudden death of her daughter and remained there for the remainder of the war years. She changed her spiritual beliefs and became a Christian Scientist and was eventually repatriated as a German citizen back to Germany. Jessie died in November 1954 in Hanover after refusing medical treatment which could have saved her life.

Jessie Jordan - Crown Copyright - Licence attained 2021 National Archives Kew

Duncan Macpherson, from Dundee, clearly recollects his parents talking about Jessie. As a child he used to play underneath the kitchen table, hidden out of sight by the tablecloth. Now nothing remains of Jessie Jordan, except stories about her notorious deceptive lifestyle – quite inconceivable that this rather ordinary woman could have caused unimaginable destruction and loss of life should her actions have been more effective.

114

ARBROATH'S NOTORIOUS ARISTOCRAT

'Absolute power corrupts absolutely….Great men are almost always bad men. *-Lord Aston*

Whilst Britain was bracing itself against the impending threat of WWII, one Conservative politician was harbouring Nazi-sympathies publicly, showing no hint of patriotism for his country. That man was Archibald Henry Maule Ramsay, a descendent of the 12th Earl of Dalhousie.

Archibald Ramsay - Crown Copyright - Licence attained 2021 from National Portrait Gallery

Born in 1894 into a Scottish aristocratic family, young Ramsay was raised in the privileged lifestyle assigned to only a few. His great uncle was a Scottish Earl and that level of family connection enabled him to attend the prestigious boarding school, Eton College. Ramsay then graduated in

1913 as an officer from the Royal Military College, Sandhurst, with his initial posting being the Coldstream Guards. When WWI commenced in 1914, Ramsay's regiment was one of the first to face life in the trenches. Like many units, his suffered vast numbers of casualties and deaths. In 1916, Ramsay suffered a severe head wound and was returned to England to recuperate. This ended his military duties at the Western Front, but he continued army service by taking up a position at the War Office.

Here he met The Honourable Ismay Lucretia, recent widow of Lord Ninian Crichton-Stuart and daughter of Viscount Gormanston and they were married on 30 April 1917. They shared one common trait – they were both passionate anti-Semites. Ramsay retired from the Army with the rank of Captain in 1920, then the family moved to Scotland.

They enjoyed the luxury of living in gothic Kelly Castle which lies within a secluded estate at Arbroath, making it their family home whilst retaining a fashionable London residence in South Kensington. Now a company director with a firm in Arbroath, he became interested in politics and became particularly outspoken against the new Russian government's philosophy on communism. At the 1931 general election he was elected as the Scottish Unionist Member of Parliament for the South Midlothian and Peebles constituency. Ramsay became increasingly right-wing in his political thinking being particularly anti-communist with his views being sympathetic to the Nazi-German regime. Largely his time during the 1930's was spent being an enthusiastic supporter of the Nationalists led by General Francisco Franco during the Spanish Civil War in 1937.

At an address to the Arbroath Business Club in 1938, he debated about the leader Adolph Hitler's sweeping hatred of the Jews. Ramsay had become increasingly sympathetic towards the German leader's theories. By 1939, the Right Honourable Ismay Ramsay also made her radical views known at a speech at the Arbroath Business Club.

Ramsay established a secret society known as The Right Club, where high-profile British fascists gathered prior to the commencement of hostilities against Germany. Associates included William Joyce the infamous Lord Haw-Haw, Sir Oswald Mosely the leader of the Blackshirts and many other notable individuals such as the Duke of Wellington, Duke of Westminster and Earl of Portsmouth. Complete membership details were held in the Red Book which was used by security agencies using the intelligence held within as well as secret documents and communications.

MI5 agents infiltrated the inner circle of the Right Club and established that an imminent fascist rebellion was being developed with its members infiltrating government departments, police and armed forces. Their treachery would aid Nazi Germany by inflicting significant damage to Britain and her allies. Espionage and treachery were found to be flourishing within the highest echelons of society with Ramsay now recognised and anticipated as being Hitler's leader for Scotland.

Ramsay was arrested in May 1940 and interned in Brixton Prison under fierce protest. His argument that his detention as a MP was a breach of his parliamentary privileges, was overruled. An appeal went before the Advisory Committee where he sought release with eventual restitution to the House of Commons. This too was overruled.

Ultimately, he was released in 1944 and did not contest his constituency seat, preferring to retire to his estate in Arbroath to write his autobiography The Nameless War: A History of the Events Leading up to the Second World War which was published in 1952.

To this day there are people who would hail him as a hero, however he was a man regarded as being consumed with power and hatred. It was luck rather than opportunity that he could not be found guilty of treason. Ramsay died in 1955.

RAF KINNABER – WIRELESS LISTENING INTERCEPTION AND RELAY STATION

56°44'48.53 N 2°26'54.09 W

First used for radio and radar operations in WWII, this station is located in North East Angus approximately two miles north of Montrose and lies beneath the river North Esk Railway viaduct, located close to the A92 main coastal road to Aberdeen.

RAF Kinnaber listening station - now derelict- photograph courtesy of M Craib

This listening station played a substantial part in the *'secret war'* by intercepting German radio transmissions and relaying them to Bletchley Park for de-coding. One of the major successes was the discovery that the Germans were developing missiles against which there was no defence, at Peenemunde. This intelligence led to bombing attacks on the enemy research facility which undoubtedly saved many allied lives.

A previous member of the Montrose Air Station Heritage Centre, David Oswald, could recollect his time working at Kinnaber. He joined the RAF in 1939 and trained as a radio operator. Initially he was sent to France with the British Expeditionary Force and was one of the survivors from that defeat and subsequent evacuation from Saint Nazaire. David was then posted to RAF Montrose where his vital radio skills were put to use at the listening post at Kinnaber where German transmissions were monitored round the clock with intercepted messages being relayed directly to Bletchley Park.

Bletchley Park - WWII Code-breaking Centre – Wikimedia Commons/Public Domain

Intelligence gathering on enemy positions, movements and plans was crucial to the Allies and the Germans, much having been collected by use of subterfuge using agents or spies, with the north-east coastal area being no exception. David recollects one of his colleagues being arrested for collating information about the number of pilots being trained at Montrose – vital information which would have been very useful to the Luftwaffe. Intercepting and de-coding German radio traffic was a more efficient method on collecting intelligence about enemy activities and there can be no doubt that British surveillance played a substantial role in the eventual victory of WWII.

David played a major role in the crucial communication plan with the Norwegian Resistance Movement – codenamed 'VERA' by receiving messages and relaying the critical information onwards. He was honoured for his service for his vital contribution in assisting Norway's liberty from German occupation, by receiving a Norwegian medal at a presentation at Montrose Air Station Heritage Centre in 2016. Sadly, David died in April 2018, but is fondly remembered by his friends and colleagues at Montrose.

Lucy Stewart, a WAAF working at Kinnaber, spoke fluent German therefore her linguistic skills were invaluable. She was one of a team of military and civilian operators who were drafted in to listen and relay information from enemy transmissions. Life, although difficult at this time, appeared to be fairly pleasant at Kinnaber with a great sense of camaraderie between the staff as their annual Christmas publication, 'The Kinnaber Rag,' illustrates.

The Kinnaber Rag – photograph courtesy of Montrose Air Station Heritage Centre

Kinnaber remained operational well into the post-war period and the facility was eventually taken over by the USN as a Microwave Relay Station associated with the directional finding and monitoring station at RAF Edzell. It operated and was maintained by USN personnel until its closure in 1977.

Today, the building remains surrounded by the military fencing at the site with many of the signs of previous occupation still evident plus the vast electrical input into the facility indicating this was a site which had the requirement for an enormous power source. The aerial masts are long gone now yet their holding posts still exist. The facility still retains an air of mystique around its situation close to the viaduct over which once ran the main London to Aberdeen rail line. The structure suffered some heavy gun fire from marauding enemy aircraft during the hostilities. Shrapnel marks and bullet holes in the Victorian viaduct which remain in the brickwork of the structure are consistent with German attack.

CHAPTER 15

RELATED MILITARY FACILITIES

AULDBAR – WWI AIRSHIP MOORING SITE

Satellite Station for RAF Montrose and RAF Longside, Peterhead, Aberdeenshire for use by RNAS Airships between 1916 and 1918

56°40'41.92 N 2°44'12.43 W

Auldbar is situated inland, south of Letham, and on the road towards Aberlemmo and Brechin. It had a busy railway junction and the airship mooring base was situated approximately 3 miles north from this point. The site was used by the newly established RAF some months prior to the end of WWI by No 22 (Operations) Group No 78 Wing, as a satellite to RAF Longside.

Auldbar Signal Box – Photograph -Writer's Own – taken in 2018

The remit for Auldbar, was to provide a mooring site for non-rigid airships when the strong north-easterly winds prevented a return to their home base. Longside, also known as 'Lenabo' was established in 1916 and remained operational until 1920. Airships from this station and Montrose would have patrolled the shipping lanes across the northernmost parts of Scotland and the North Sea coastal fringes. Invariably, weather conditions blew the airships off course which led to the necessity for having an additional landing site further south and inland where the airships could be moored safely.

There were no sheds or hangars used at Auldbar, instead four large depressions known as *nests* were developed amidst the forest area of adjacent Montreathment, where the airships could be moored for shelter, relatively unseen. Recorded *Landing Grounds* used during WWI were often just a field with tented accommodation for service personnel from the Home Defence Squadron. This was exactly the arrangement at Auldbar, used for a short time by a skeleton team before the site was finally closed in 1919. Today, the ground indentations can be viewed easily from a height and some of the mooring blocks are still visible as a reminder of their important function.

The function of these huge and difficult to manage structures in certain weather conditions, was fairly short lived, whilst the capabilities of the aeroplane, designed to be a successful fighting force, advanced rapidly over the following years.

The superiority of the aeroplane over the airship was raised in the House of Commons in 1915 by Winston Churchill, MP, [1] who stated, '*Panic may resent it; ignorance may deride it; malice may distort it; but there it is.*'

The time of the airship was finally over.

HMS CONDOR II - RNAS STANNERGATE - SEAPLANES

56° 27'53.45 N 2°55'01.93 W

Situated on the Firth of Tay at Dundee and close to the Angus military airfields, Dundee Stannergate saw longer service in the 20th century than *any other seaplane base in Scotland*. Established in early 1914, prior to the start of WWI, and at the command of the First Lord of the Admiralty (1911-1915), Winston Churchill, (MP for Dundee at the time), it was one of the many air bases along the east coast with which the RNAS could protect the movements of the Home Fleet.

In 1912 the Kendal Mercury Times reported Churchill 'authorised a Naval Wing of the Flying Corps to use aircraft for harbour, estuary, coastal defence also scouting.' The military then developed a hydro-aeroplane called 'Waterbird', Britain's first successful float plane. Churchill, fascinated by the innovation informed Ministers in the House of Commons that 'results so far attained had been promising.' He also claimed credit for the term *seaplane* at a House of Commons hearing in 1913 whilst keeping a 'hands-on approach to defence'.

In Dundee, the Admiralty leased a large area of reclaimed land on the Tay estuary and the first operational aircraft was a *Borel Hydroplane* which arrived on the 9th February 1914. These seaplanes undertook reconnaissance missions and patrols for convoys routes being vigilant for enemy submarines operating in the North Sea. By 1916, there were eight seaplanes at the base which was built over two adjacent sites dissected by the main London to Aberdeen railway line.

WWI Naval Seaplane on submarine spotting mission – Wikimedia Commons/Public Domain

On the shore side, there were initially two seaplane sheds, which was increased to four as the war progressed. There were also technical buildings with two slipways leading directly into the Tay. On the north side of the railway line, there was a large camp which contained buildings and accommodation for the several hundred personnel who were based there. This site also had its own *carrier pigeon service* which was vital for communication at that time. A powerful wireless station was added at a later time. The officers' accommodation and wardroom were located in a large private villa situated off the current Broughty Ferry Road named *The Wick*.

Among the *characters* stationed at Stannergate, was *flying ace - Squadron Commander Christopher Draper*, who will be remembered for flying seaplanes back and forth through the spans of the Tay Rail Bridge which spans the River Tay from Wormit in Fife to Dundee. He earned the nickname of *The Mad Major* for performing his dare-devil antics, one of which was when ordered to land an aircraft on the green at St Andrews Golf Course, he stopped directly right in front of the Clubhouse. Perhaps known best for his *stunts* he became a film star in the post war period plying his aviation skills for the movie-makers, yet in the 1930's he operated as a British secret agent, serving as a double agent to Germany. At the outbreak of WWII, he was back to see action with the Fleet Air Arm.

In 1918, the base was home to *No 249 and No 257 Squadrons with Felixstowe F2A flying* boats *and Admiralty Short 184 seaplanes,* for patrols and defence purposes with the third hangar having been erected, which was of much larger dimensions to accommodate these. Classified as *an F-type Hangar,* this all-metal construction was made by *Frodingham Iron and Steel Company.* In the same year, Dundee Stannergate was utilised as an *acceptance station* for new seaplanes delivered directly from manufacturers to be tested. 'G Flight' – Boat Seaplane Training (BST) operated here from mid-August 1918 until 1919. The active services eventually disbanded in 1919 and the station closed down in 1920.

The main part of the site was then sold to individual companies for industrial usage, the camp accommodation dismantled, and *the H-shaped brick buildings* present were used as post-war housing before ultimately being demolished.

The spring of 1940 saw WWII now in progress and the need for Stannergate to reopen by the RNAS for active duties, this time as HMS Condor II, the satellite station for HMS Condor at Arbroath, located further up the north-east coast. This was the base for *Walrus Flying boats of 751 Detachment and the Vought Kingfishers of 703 Squadron* operating on pilot training with a sixty-foot slipway in operation. This led from shore to hangars with three, twenty-five feet dispersal tracks leading out from the hangar apron. During this time the air station at Arbroath was at capacity, the pace of the war was intensifying and RNAS East Haven was coming on line. Arbroath's Seaplane School for Observer Training moved to Dundee in August 1941 and remained there until 1944. Catapult crews also underwent a 10-week course of which 3 weeks were spent at Dundee.

Activity increased rapidly on the Stannergate site with No *751 Squadron* operating from August 1941, with catapult training for observer crews in *Supermarine Walrus amphibians* continuing until 1944. Around this time *Vought-Sikorsky Kingfisher floatplanes* from *703 Squadron* were also operating from this base.

A *Gunnery School* for *defensively equipped merchant ships* (DEMS) operated in the harbour close to Stannergate with a WRNS training establishment rapidly set up in a building what was previously known as *Mathers Hotel.* Wireless Operators for both Royal and the Merchant Navy were trained at the Dundee Wireless College at 40 Windsor Street off the Perth Road, near to the city centre. Dundee was prepared for war and ready for action.

On the 12 February at 10.28 a Junkers 88 on an anti-shipping raid was shot down by naval gunfire crashing in Pitairlie Wood near the village of Newbigging. The crew of four were killed and two unexploded bombs were found.

In her published memoir, Margaret Gilles Brown recollects '*Dundee being bombed on the 2ⁿᵈ August 1940*' and also viewing '*a lot of German activity especially offshore when German aircraft and floatplanes laid mines and attacked shipping. Sporadic bombing was taking place all around our coastline. After Germany took over Norway, they operated raids from Stavanger and ships around Dundee were an easy target.'* She also remembers *'getting used to the air-raid sirens with their long wail and welcomed the relief of the all clear'.*

Kay Landsburgh also remembers the air shelters at the bottom of her family's garden and the little knitted 'Churchill Siren Suit' that most of the young children wore for the duration of the air raids.

David Lowson, now at one hundred years of age and a direct descendent of Tammas Lowson who was the founder of Carnoustie, clearly recollects Dundee at war as if it was yesterday. In a reserved occupation working in the Blackness Foundry, David remembers one evening walking home to Rosefield Street and hearing the noise of the German bombers coming over the city and the noise of the bombs falling. He ran to take shelter against the stone wall of the local school and felt the blast resonate as buildings in his street were demolished. He remembers clearly on the night of the 5th November 1940 a bomb being dropped on number 17, the tenement building opposite and seeing the wallpaper and pictures still intact on the remaining walls.

Rosefield Street Dundee 1940 - Photograph courtesy of Pinterest

Thirty eight bombs were reported to fall over the city of Dundee during WWII but these stats take no account of the number of missiles which came down in the Tay nor the vast number of mines that were washed up on the coastal beaches some of which are still being found today and dealt with by Bomb Disposal Teams from Leuchars. The most recent in 2020 at the beach in Carnoustie, dealt with by a controlled explosion.

RNAS Stannergate reduced to Care and Maintenance on the 15th June 1944 and finally closed shortly after, unfortunately, there are no surviving military structures left. When the military had no further use for the site, it became a successful General Aviation airfield for a time operating as 'Dundee Airport' with one single asphalt runway and managed by the city council but used primarily by private owners. The land thereafter became part of Dundee's harbour area and the ground between, what originally was the two slipways, was filled in. Another example of a busy military base that has gradually disappeared from our landscape.

HERITAGE INFORMATION

The World Record for the longest seaplane uninterrupted seaplane flight took place on 6th October 1938 from the River Tay, Dundee by Captain DC Bennett (later to establish the RAF Pathfinder Force during WWII) and his First Officer, Ian Hanley. The Maia Empire Flying Boat took off from the Tay with the Mercury seaplane on its shoulders. This 'piggy-back' method of launching aircraft was called 'Mayo Composite' after Major Robert Mayo of Imperial Airways who devised the technique. The two planes separated over Dundee Law then proceeded to fly 6045 miles in Mercury in 42 hours 26 minutes. The finishing point was the Orange River estuary at Alexander Bay South Africa as the aircraft had insufficient fuel to reach its intended destination of Cape Town due to adverse weather conditions.

Sandra Ireland, an acclaimed Angus author, recollects her mother telling her of the day when she had been allowed an extended lunch break from her workplace to go down to the river to watch the take off. It was a momentous occasion for the people of Dundee, who flocked down to the riverside to watch the event. Maia, the larger and more powerful of the two and Mercury above, were manufactured by the Short Brothers for Imperial Airways, with the aim of getting an aircraft with a heavy payload being launched airborne from a short take-off run.

Mercury above Maia - Photograph by National Library of Ireland on Wikimedia Commons/ Public Domain

Sadly, neither seaplane survived WWII. Maia was destroyed during an air-raid at Poole whilst Mercury was broken up for aluminium at Rochester, however they are immortalised in the city of Dundee with the Airport being situated at Mayo Avenue and a commemorative plaque describing the event of 1938 placed on the riverside walkway.

ACKNOWLEDGEMENTS

Without the assistance of the following individuals, my task in writing about the Lost Airfields of Angus, would have been impossible and far less interesting.

In particular, I thank Alan Doe (Chairman 2001-2017), Stuart Archibald current Chairman, Dan Paton Curator and the dedicated volunteers at Montrose Air Station Heritage Centre. They are all amazing and talented people.

I am especially indebted to Michael Craib for sharing his exceptional photography and Ron Woomble, my proof reader and advisor – you are both true military enthusiasts and have provided remarkable guidance and support.

I was privileged to be escorted around RM Condor by Lt Alexander Saunders, RN, who selflessly dedicated an afternoon driving me around the airfield, allowing me the opportunity to take appropriate photographs.

Special thanks go to Gary Archer, Training Safety Officer (MOD) and Phil Abramson, Archaeologist at Defence Infrastructure Organisation (DIO) who allowed me access to meet with the archaeology team of Wessex Archaeology on their excavations of WWI trenches and WWII turret at Barry Buddon Camp, Carnoustie.

I owe so much to Gillian Duff, Ann Craig, and Betty Doe, all former Presidents and current members of Angus Writers' Circle, also to Eric Yeaman and the wonderful members of Tay Writers in Dundee for their encouragement and literary expertise. It was worth it guys.

My sincere thanks go to Angus artist Rikki Craig for his creative cover design and to Bruce Clark, Printers, Dundee whose skills have made this publication so attractive. Thanks also go to Frank Duncan and Oliver Kelly for the page layout design.

Grateful thanks go to Dundee Local History Archive staff, Dundee Museum of Transport and Angus Archives and Library Services, the National Archives at Kew and the National Portrait Gallery for assisting me with research and photographic material.

To my very dear friend, Jane White, who almost got us both arrested for taking photographs of the old runway at Edzell, thank you for your patience and holding your nerve!

Finally, I would thank my husband Michael and sons, Jonathan and Richard who have always had faith in my determination to succeed.

Margaret G. Bowman

2021

REFERENCE LIST +
BIBLIOGRAPHY SOURCES

Ackroyd, J.A.D. (2011) *Sir George Cayley: The Invention of the Aeroplane near Scarborough at the time of Trafalgar.* pp.130-180. London: Journal of Aeronautical History

Armitage, M. (1993) *The Royal Air Force: An Illustrated History.* London: Arms & Armour

Adlam, H. (2007) *On and Off the Flight Deck.* Barnsley: Pen and Sword

Anderson, D. (1998) *The World at War 1939-45.* London: Toucan

Angus Writers' Anthology, (2007) *About Angus pp. 26-27.* Brechin: City Press

Barclay, G. (2013) *If Hitler Comes.* Edinburgh: Birlinn

Belati, M. (2015) *The Zeppelin.* Barnsley: Pen and Sword

Black, C. (2004) *Franklin Delano Roosevelt: Champion of Freedom.* London: Phoenix

Blair, A.W. and Smith, A. (2015) *The Pioneer Flying Achievements of Preston Watson.* Elgin: Librario

Bowman, M.G. (2018) *Paying Homage in the Highlands.* pp. 30-31 London: Best of British Magazine

Bowyer, C. (1983) *Bomber Barons.* Barnsley: Pen and Sword

Breuer, W.B. (2001) *Daring Missions of WWII.* Canada: Wiley and Sons

Brown, M.G. (2016) *A Rowan Tree in My Garden.* Forfar: Robertson

Churchill, W.S. (1933) *The Great War Vol I-III.* London: Clowes and Sons

Cochrane, J. (1998) *A Fragile Peace 1919-39.* London: Toucan

Dawes, L. (2016) *Fighting Fit: The Wartime Battle for Britain's Health.* London: Orion

Delve, K. (2010) *The Military Airfields of Britain; Scotland and Northern Ireland.* London: Marlborough

Ferguson, N. (2016) *From Airbus to Zeppelin.* Gloucester: History Press

Ferrier, W. (2015) *The Well 'Read' Lichtie.* UK:Unknown

Francis, P. (1996) *British Military Airfield Architecture.* Somerset: Haynes

Good Housekeeping. (2005) *Wartime Scrapbook.* London: Collins

Grossman, Gauze and Russell, (2017) *Zeppelin Hindenberg: an illustrated history of LZ-129.* Gloucester: History Press

Hamilton, J.A.B. (1967) *Britain's Railways in WWI.* London: Unwin

Hammerton, J.A. (None) *A Popular History of the Great War Vol I-VI.* London: Fleetway

Harris, C. (2003) *Women at War in Uniform 1939-1945.* Gloucester: Sutton

Harris, R. (1995) *Enigma.* London: Hutchison

Hastings, M. (2009) *Finest Years. Churchill as Warhead 1940-1945.* London: Harper Press

Healey,T. (1993) *Life on the Home Front; Journeys into the Past.* London: Toucan

Holmes, R. (2009) *Churchill's Bunker.* London: Profile

Inglis, F. (2010) *Phantoms and Fairies: Tales of the Supernatural in Angus and Dundee.* Brechin: Pinkfoot Press

Ingram, J.R. (2013) *Whither Wings?* Oxford: Marston

Innes, G.B. (1995) *British Airfield Buildings of the Second World War. Aviation Pocket Guide.* London: Allan

Jeffrey, A. (1991) *This Dangerous Menace: Dundee and the River Tay at War 1939-1945.* Edinburgh: Mainstream

Jeffreys-Jones, R. (2013) *In Spies We Trust.* Oxford: University Press

McIntyre, B. (2014) *A Spy Among Friends.* London: Bloomsbury

McIntyre, D.F. (1936) *The Pilot's Book of Everest.* London: Hodge

McKinstry, L. (2020) *Hurricaine. Victor of the Battle of Britain.* London: Murray

Montefiore, S.S. (2010) *Speeches That Changed the World*. London: Quercus

Neil, T. (2006) *Flight into Darkness*. Walton on Thames: Air Research Publications

Neil, T. (2003) *The Silver Spitfire*. London: Nicholson

Neil, T. (2010) *Gun Button to Fire; A Hurricane Pilots Dramatic Story of the Battle of Britain*. Stroud: Amberley

Nicol, L. (2018) *The Great War: Dundee and the Home Front*. Dundee: City Archives

Readers Digest ((1996) *Yesterdays Britain*. UK: Readers Digest

Pidgeon, G. (2003) The Secret Wireless War; The Story of MI6 Communications 1939-1945.

UK: Arundel

Richardson, E.H. (1920) *British War Dogs: Their Training and Psychology*. London: Skeffington & Sons

Richardson, E.H. (1929) *Forty Years with Dogs*. London: Hutchison

Riley, J.F. (1957) *The First Flying Scot*. The Meccano Magazine Vol XLII No 6 pp. 284-5

Sarkar, D. (2010) *Spitfire Voices*. Gloucester: Amberley

Smith, D.J. (1983) *Action Stations 7: Military Airfields of Scotland, the North East and Northern Ireland*. Cambridge: Stephens

Smith, D.J. (1989) *Britain's Military Airfields 1939-45*. Cambridge: Stephens

Smith, L. and Paton, D. (2001) *Learning to Fly at Montrose: RFC/RAF Montrose: The Story in Words and Pictures 1913-1950*. UK: Ian McIntosh Memorial Trust

Smith, M. (2000) *Britain in 1940*. London: Routledge

Stelzer, C. (2011) *Dinner with Churchill*. London: Short

Stewart, G. (2019) *Sergeant Thomas Brown – Aviation Pioneer: First Flight to India 1919*. UK: Unknown

Sutcliffe, J.A. (1992) *The Sayings of Winston Churchill.* London: Duckworth

Tate, T. (2018) *Hitler's British Traitors.* London: Icon

Uhlig, R. (2010) *Genius of Britain: The Scientists who Changed the World.* London: Collins

White, J. (2008) *Endgame: The U-Boat Inshore Campaign.* Gloucester: History Press

Williams, G. and Roetter, C. (1954) *The Wit of Winston Churchill.* London: Parrish

Willmot, H.P. Cross, R. and Messenger, C. (2014) *World War II.* London: Dorling Kimberley

PUBLICATIONS

A Brief History of the Royal Air Force (2004) RAF Publications.

Aviation- A Historical Survey from its origins to the end of WWII. (1970) C.H. Gibbs-Smith, HMSO for The Science Museum, London

The Zeppelins at War – The National Archives

WWI Audit of Surviving Remains. Project (GJB) 31.3.13 HS/RCA HMSO

Dundee Courier & Advertiser; The Courier – D.C. Thomson Publications

ON-LINE PUBLICATIONS

RAF Schoolhill – Chain Home Radar Station. (2015) Nick Catford: Subterranea.Britannica. www.subbrit.org.uk

Documenting Decay. www.derelictplaces.co.uk

War in the Air. www.thefirstworldwar.com

WW2 German bombing of HMS Condor. www.secretscotland.com – RNAS Arbroath

Engineering Timelines. www.flyingmachines.org

Airships. www.airshipsonline.com

Tealing Village. www.tealing.com

FILM PRODUCTIONS

Enigma – Released September 2001 - UK

Those Magnificent Men in their Flying Machines – Released 1965 - USA

Wings Over Everest – Released November 2019

Darkest Hour – Released January 2018

ORGANISATIONS

RNAS Yeovilton Somerset. www.fleetairarm.com

RAF Museum Cosford Shifnal. www.raf.com

Imperial War Museum London. www.imperialwarmuseum.com

TELEVISION

The Daredevils who Flew Across an Ocean. Dan Box www.bbc.co.uk

PO Box 25. The RSS from 1939-45. BBC News 24th July 2004

HMS Ambrose. BBC News 16th September 2009

Montrose Air Station Heritage Drama written by Elizabeth Doe – 2016 – centenary event

ABOUT THE AUTHOR

Margaret Bowman is an award- winning writer who lives in rural Angus, central to the war time military airfields.

She is Vice President also Press Secretary for Angus Writers' Circle and is their representative to the Scottish Association of Writers, also Secretary for Tay Writers, Dundee and the Press Secretary for the Friends of Carnoustie and District Heritage.

Works which include historical features and poetry have been published in various magazine publications and anthologies in the UK. She was awarded the Christie Trophy for outstanding contribution by Angus Writers in 2019 and the Eastwood Silver Salver in 2020 by the Scottish Association of Writers.

'The Lost Airfields of Angus' received prizewinning awards by the Scottish Association of Writers in 2020 and 2021.

Index

C

D

LUSITANIA 8

ORFORD NESS 98–99

OSWALD, DAVID 116, 118

P

PARACHUTES 15

PEEWIT, HMS 11, 44, 54, 56–57

PETERHEAD 10, 29, 62, 83, 85, 122

PICKETT-HAMILTON FORT 20

Q

QUARTERS 12, 14, 17, 19, 107

R

RADAR 20, 34, 45, 53, 86, 96–103, 118

RADIO SECURITY SERVICE 105

RAMSAY, ARCHIBALD 115–117

RAMSAY, ISMAY 115–117

RED LICHTIE 22, 38

RICHARDSON, EDWIN 92–93

ROCKING RING SYSTEM 4

ROYAL AERO CLUB 5, 25

ROYAL FLYING CORPS 6, 8

ROYAL NAVAL AIR SERVICE 5, 8

S

SEAPLANES 105, 124–126